PR̶ ̶ ̶ ̶ ̶ ̶
IN
VISION

Building a Process-Driven Organization

The AG Business Flow Framework™

Arun Govindaraj

Estimation & Commercial Operations Leader
Oil & Gas | Petrochemical | Power | Fabrication Services

AG Publications

Published by AG Publications

ISBN:

Disclaimer: This book reflects personal professional experiences
and general best practices. It does not disclose proprietary or
confidential information of any organization. References to
standards such as PMBOK®, AACE®, or ISO® are for educational
purposes only.

Note: All case studies, examples, and scenarios described in this
book are created for illustrative and educational purposes. While
they are inspired by real professional experiences, they do not
depict any specific company, project, or individual. Any
resemblance to actual events or personas, living or deceased, is
purely coincidental.

For more information, please visit
https://www.linkedin.com/in/arungovindarajtrichy

To my wife Karthika and my daughter Poojasri, for their constant encouragement and belief in this journey. And to my little son Ajay, who quietly supported me by letting me work in peace while I completed this book.

ACKNOWLEDGEMENTS

Writing this book has been a journey shaped by many people and experiences.

I am deeply thankful to my mentors, colleagues, and the leaders I have worked under during my years across fabrication and service industries in Oil & Gas, Petrochemical, and Power sectors. Each project, discussion, and challenge added to the ideas that became the AG Business Flow Framework™.

My gratitude extends to my previous employers and who trusted me with responsibilities that tested both my discipline and creativity. Their guidance built the foundation that allowed this book to take form.

A special appreciation also goes to the new wold of AI, for helping refine my thoughts, edit complex ideas, and structure to years of real-world experience. It turned practical lessons into knowledge could be shared with precision and clarity.

To my parents, Father Govindaraj and Mother Vijayalakshmi, thank you for teaching me the values of discipline, integrity, and perseverance that guided every step of this journey.

And, as always to my family, Karthika, Poojasri, and little Ajay, thank you for standing beside me with patience, belief, and love throughout this entire journey.

TABLE OF CONTENT

Purpose of This Book

The purpose of this book is to show that reliability in any organization is not built by chance or by individual effort alone. It is built by process, discipline, and clarity of intention.

Across industries, whether in fabrication, maintenance, or service, many teams work hard yet struggle to achieve consistent results. This happens not because people lack skill but because their systems lack rhythm.

Precision in Vision: Building a Process-Driven Organization was written to bridge that gap. It introduces the **AG Business Flow Framework**^{TM}**,** a structured model that connects leadership, estimation, execution, finance, and foresight into one continuous flow of reliability.

This book is for leaders, engineers, and professionals who want to turn experience into systems and systems into sustainable performance. It is also for those who believe that process is not paperwork but the translation of purpose into daily action.

If it helps you build even one system that runs more smoothly, one decision that becomes clearer, or one team that learns to trust its own process, then its purpose is fulfilled.

Chapter 1: From Vision to Value - The DNA of a Process-Driven Company

AG Business Flow Framework™

"Reliability isn't a trait. It's a design."

1. The Purpose Behind Every Process

Every strong company begins with a purpose. Not just a contract or a profit target, but an intent that reaches deeper to build something that lasts.

Across industries, whether in service or manufacturing, the common purpose is reliability. Clients depend on organizations that can deliver consistent results even when the pressure is high. It might mean machining a valve body to micron accuracy or assembling a shutdown crew overnight.

Reliability does not happen by chance. It is built through process, through a deliberate chain of actions designed to work the same way every time, no matter who performs them. A company that truly lives by process does not depend on memory or personality. It depends on clarity.

In reality, the value chain begins long before the first pipe spool is cut or the first invoice is raised. It begins the moment a potential opportunity is recognized. That is when market intelligence, relationships, and capability quietly align to create a new possibility. From that point onward, every stage that follows, including estimation, execution, billing, and finance, form a continuous flow of value creation.

*Insight: **A process is not paperwork. It is the translation of vision into everyday behaviour.***

When processes weaken, even strong teams struggle. A missing quotation can stall a bid. A lost approval can hold an entire project in limbo. Every gap in documentation or communication costs time, money, and sometimes credibility. One real incident from a shutdown project in a petrochemical plant proved this clearly. A single missing document kept an entire operation waiting for hours.

2. People-Dependent vs. Process-Dependent Organizations

Aspect	People-Dependent	Process-Dependent
Knowledge Flow	Stored in memory and experience	Documented, repeatable, auditable
Decision Making	Driven by hierarchy or intuition	Guided by data and workflow
Risk Profile	High, success varies by person	Low, success repeats by system
Scalability	Limited to individual capacity	Scales through structure
Continuity	Vulnerable to turnover	Sustained through documentation

A process-driven company is not emotionless. It is emotionally disciplined. It protects its people by reducing dependence on them and allows talent to strengthen systems rather than replace them.

***Leadership Reflection:** When process becomes habit, excellence becomes normal.*

Case Study: The Lost Dossier

During a critical shutdown at petrochemical plant, a pressure vessel underwent a modification that required ASME "R"-Stamp repair certification. The repair itself was executed flawlessly. The welders were qualified, the WPS was approved, and the NDT results were fully verified. After inspection, the Authorised Inspector reviewed and signed Form R-1, the Report of Repair, officially certifying the work.

It should have been a moment of closure. Yet when the final dossier was compiled for submission, the signed R-1 form was missing. Somewhere between the QC desk, operations, and document control, the paper trail simply broke.

It was not theft or negligence. It was a failure of handover and recording. The signed form had changed hands without acknowledgement, no receipt noted, no digital entry made. When the QC coordinator checked the dossier log, the most critical document, the signed R-1 Form, was untraceable.

Without that form, the vessel could not be legally recommissioned. The Authorised Inspector refused to issue a duplicate without full re-verification, and the plant's start-up was delayed for 2 days. Technically, the job was flawless. Procedurally, it was a failure.

That incident left a lasting truth. **Urgency can fix today, but process prevents tomorrow**.

> **Leadership Reflection:** *The real loss was not the document itself. It was the trust in the process. The missing record exposed a quiet weakness. People completed their tasks, but no one owned the information flow. In high-stakes operations, document control is not clerical work. It is operational continuity. That experience became a cornerstone for defining how reliability must institutionalised rather than improvised.*

3. Introducing the AG Business Flow Framework™

Every business that wants to be successful for a long time goes through natural stages of process evolution, from the first RFQ from a client to the final payment. You can never reach true excellence by only doing well in one department. It grows from a series of precise connections.

Over the years, I transformed these lessons into the **AG Business Flow Framework**, a 5-step model that turns organizations that respond to problems into ones that can forecast and support themselves.

- **Lead Discipline:** Making sales and opportunity management clearer.
- **Estimation Accuracy:** Turning scope into value and trust.
- **Execution Control:** Turning plans into results that can be measured.
- **Financial Integrity:** Making sure that every dollar earned is actually received.
- **Predictive Maturity:** Putting foresight and digital sustainability into practice.

Every step makes the one before it stronger. Sales creates good chances. Estimation turns those chances become real obligations. Execution gives you results you can measure. Finance makes sure that work pays off. Then, predictive maturity lets the whole cycle learn, change, and get better on its own.

These five steps work together to build a single plan for progress. They show every organization how to go from being dependent on people to being fully process-driven. You will see these phases in every chapter of this book, from sales discipline to digital transformation. Each one shows a link in the chain of value creation.

Discipline is not the same as constraint. It is a steady beat.

4. Leadership Mindset for Lead Discipline

The first test of leadership is not crisis management. **It is clarity creation**. Leaders who demand speed without defining process create motion without direction. Those who establish clarity early prevent confusion later.

Lead Discipline is the art of aligning intent with information. It is about knowing not only what to pursue, but also why and how to pursue it. The foundation of this discipline lies in one simple behaviour: **consistency before complexity**.

> *Leadership Insight*: Urgency fixes today. Process prevents tomorrow.

5. The Change from Work to Alignment

A lot of companies still think that hard work leads to more work. More meetings, longer hours, and quicker replies. But true performance doesn't come from just trying hard. It comes from being aligned.

When sales, estimation, operations, and finance all use the same data and concepts, work becomes more efficient, and efficiency leads to excellence.

Alignment makes ensuring that each function helps the next one instead of completing for urgency. It changes single actions into a collective structure, which helps the organization go from being reactive to being predictive.

6. The Seed of Predictive Maturity

All mature organisation start off as a disciplined one. Predictive maturity does not appear overnight. It grows through a thousand small acts of consistency.

Checklists turn become into dashboards. Dashboards turn into insights. Insights turn into foresight.

At that stage, the organisation starts to think for itself. Not as a metaphor, but in practice. Its systems talk to each other, its data predicts the future, and its leadership finally have the power to lead.

> **Vision Statement**
>
> *"Leaders can lead when systems think"*

7. Reflection on the Chapter: From Vision to Flow

The **AG Business Flow Framework** was not created to give people more control. The goal was to cut down on disorder.

It changes supervision to visibility, firefighting to foresight, and urgency to rhythm.

When people are driven by purpose and process, reliability becomes second nature.

This is not paperwork. **That is freedom made achievable by structure**.

Chapter 2: Managing Sales and Opportunities

AG Business Flow Framework™

"Sales discipline is the first test of reliability."

1. Introduction: Why Discipline in Leadership is Important

Every business wants a consistent stream of orders. But dependability starts long before an order is placed. It starts from the very beginning of business process, when leads are found, screened, and either pursued or declined on purpose.

Sales discipline isn't about how quickly we send out a quote. It's about how smartly we judge each chance. This is the first serious test of the organization's legitimacy. Clients begin to believe our commitment when every lead is handled in a structured and accountable way, and our forecasts become more accurate.

Case 1: The missed Requirement for a Scaffold

A maintenance contractor rushed through a quote for refinery shutdown without checking the access scope. Once the work started, scaffolding cost took up 40% of the margin without warning.

> *Leadership Lesson: Qualification is a better approach to safeguard profit than negotiating.*

2. Sales as the First Line of Defence

Sales isn't just a department. It is the first line of defence for the reliability of an organization. It tells the difference between noise and real intent and turns market opportunities into initiatives that can be done. In industries that are driven by processes, sales are both technical and consultative, balancing potential with deliverability.

Primary responsibilities

- Use networks, portals, and market data to find opportunities that fit with your goals.
- Check the scope, capability, and profitability before making any promises.
- Work closely with the teams in charge of estimating, operations, finance, and procurement.
- Put market data into dashboards so that leaders can make predictions.
- Keep in touch with clients after they win a deal to build a good long-term reputation.

Case 2: Modular Thinking Gets the Job

A fabrication company saw that an EPC client was having trouble with server site congestion. The sales engineer suggested modular pre-fabrication, which cut the time it took to put up the building by 35%. The proposal was so good that it led to three contracts in a row.

> **Takeaway for Leaders:** *Fix things before you sell them. Understanding comes before value.*

3. Opportunity Identification and Predicting Accuracy

Disciplined identification makes sure that sales pipelines are realistic instead of becoming wish list that are too big. For accurate forecasting, you need to filter opportunities through clear and consistent criteria:

- Technical fit

- Availability of resources
- Credibility of the client
- Potential for profit

Case 3: The missed Registering as a Vendor

A new petrochemical client asked a regional fabrication company to register as a vendor. Because there was no project that needed to be done right now, the inquiry was given low priority. Months later, the same client put out a framework tender costing millions, but only registered vendors could bid on it. The company didn't realize the link until after the submission window had closed.

> **Leadership Lesson:** *Every early request has the potential to lead to something bigger. If you ignore modest beginning, you might miss big chances.*

Sales discipline that is accurate leads to steady income. Management dashboards transform from guessing to guiding when every lead is logged, evaluated at, and maintained up to date.

4. Pre-qualification of the client

The client looks at the company's documents to see how trustworthy it is before making a bid. They look at the company's financial strength, project experience, and health and safety systems. Keeping an up-to-date, live pre-qualification database that is updated every three months shows that you are ready and honest. Before the first quote is even opened, a single expired certificate or out-of-date reference might discreetly take a company out of the business.

5. The Five-Stage Funnel and Opportunity Flow

In a process-driven organization, opportunity management follows a set pattern that turns chance into certainty. Sales discipline isn't about how many enquiries come in. It's about how consistently each one is put via structure and clarity.

In process-driven organisation, opportunity management follows a measurable rhythm that converts possibility into predictability. Sales discipline is not about how many enquires arrive. It is about how consistently each one is filtered through structure and clarity.

A glance into the Funnel

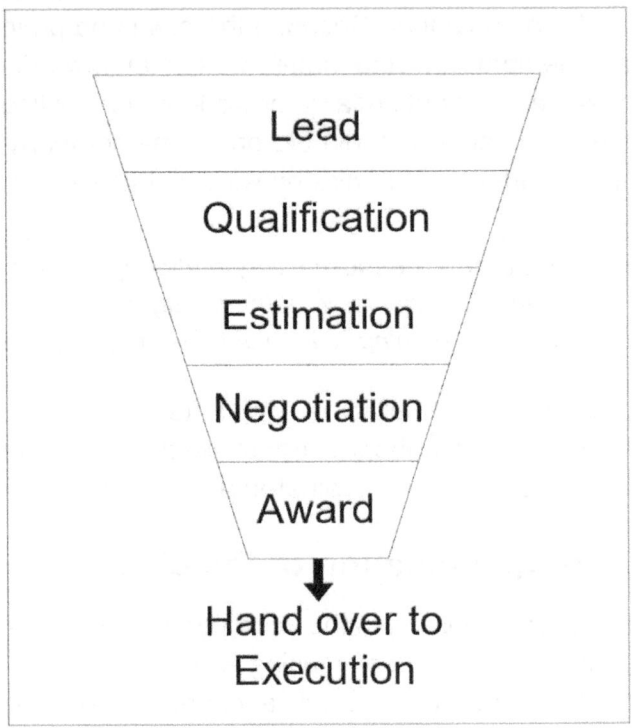

Figure 1 - Five Stage Funnel

Each stage is a point of clarity that makes sure that effort, accuracy, and alignment are stronger with each phase.

Integrated Process Flow

- **Lead Logged in CRM:** All inquiries are logged with the client's name, the scope of work, and the source of the information.
- **Qualification:** The sales staff checks to see if the opportunity is a good fit, feasible, and profitable.

- **GO/NO-GO Review**: A review that includes people from Sales, Operations, Estimation, and Management make sure that the strategy and risk are in line.

- **Estimation and Proposal Development:** The Opportunity turns into a proposal that has been costed, evaluated and backed up by data and validation.

- **Negotiation and clarification:** All parties agree on and make clear the final commercial and technical terms.

- **Award and Handover:** Winning bids are moved to execution with a full and validated handover package.

Each step makes things less uncertain, makes predictions more accurate, and turns sales activity into demonstrable organizational reliability.

Key Stage of Ownership Framework

Stage	Key Deliverable	Responsible Owner
Lead	Lead Log Entry	Sales
Qualification	Go/No-Go Evaluation and Opportunity Log Entry	Sales + Management
Estimation	Costed Proposal	Estimation
Negotiation	Clarified Scope Summary	Sales + Estimation + Operations
Award	Handover Package	Project / Execution Team

Insight: Clarity Beats Speed

A fabrication company that used this 5-stage funnel was able to minimize the time it took to get a quote from 7 days to 3.5 days. In just one quarter, the accuracy of bid forecasts went from 65% to 90%.

> ***Takeaway for Leaders:*** *Structure doesn't slow down sales. It speed up trust.*

6. Go/No-Go: The Firewall for Decisions

A systematic Go/No-Go approach protects resources and profits.

Criterion	Weight %	Score (1–5)	Weighted
Strategic Alignment	25	4	1.0
Resource Availability	20	5	1.0
Profit Potential	25	3	0.75
Risk Level	15	4	0.6
Client Credibility	15	5	0.75
Total	100		**4.1 (G o)**

Case 4: The NO-GO that Saved the Year

A workshop decided not to pursue an offer worth 1.2 million dollars after analysing the client's financial standing and reliability. The 120 day credit terms raised concern during the Go/No-Go review, and the team decided to decline. Several months later, the same client failed on larger payments to other contractors.

> ***Leadership Lesson:*** *Sometimes discipline pays off by refusing to lose.*

7. Coordination and Handover Discipline

Inside sales reliability depends on how well departments work together in rhythm.

Checklist

- Estimation: Technical details and the logic behind the prices.

- Operations: Making sure resources are ready and the timeline is in inline.

- Finance: Checking credit and review and determining bonding limits.

- Procurement: How long it takes for suppliers to deliver goods and how easy it is to get the materials you need.

- Management: Approving the strategy and signing off on the risks.

The estimation team starts the process with all the information they need, thanks to a formal sales handover package that includes the RFQ, scope, identified risks, and competitor information.

> ***Thinking about Leadership****: The hardest decision in sales is often the choice not to say "yes." Real leaders don't build credibility by chasing every opportunity. They earn it through the discipline to pursue only the right ones.*

8. Strategic Partnerships and Subcontracting

When working on big project, organizations often needed help from outside experts. This may require thrust boring, insulation, scaffolding, or specialty machining. Real sales discipline means not only qualifying client but also partners.

Early partner Identification

Engage potential subcontractors during the bidding stage rather than after the award. Early involvement allows precise pricing, schedule alignment, and technical feasibility assessments, lowering the chance of surprises later.

Clear Agreements Create Trust

Clear divisions of scope, liability, and billing milestones help keep things from getting messy and protect profits. Partnerships rarely fail because of a lack of capability. They fail because the expectations were never the same.

9. Digital Governance and CRM

Modern CRM systems act as both the company's memory and its radar. They capture every enquiry, decision, and outcome, constituting the backbone of forecast accuracy.

Benefits

- All teams can see leads in one place.
- Reminders for deadlines and renewals that are sent automatically.
- Real-time analytics on conversion and client performance.
- Integration with finance and projects for cash-flow forecasting.

When dashboards are easy to see, people are more likely to be responsible. A good CRM changes the question from "Who forgot?" to "What have we learned?" it becomes the foundation for process maturity.

10. Problems that happen frequent and ways to fix them

Sales systems that have been around for a long time still have problems that come up again and again. The difference between process-driven organizations and others is not what they don't have problems, but that they have established ways to fix them. The table below shows how discipline may turn sales problems into strong forecasts.

Problems	Root Cause	Remedy & Control Action
Incomplete RFQs	Poor client communication or unclear scope definitions	Implement Structured Clarification Templates before estimation begins.

Problems	Root Cause	Remedy & Control Action
Low-Value or Unviable Bids	Absence of Go/No-Go discipline	Apply a Qualification Matrix linking opportunity fit, margin, and resource readiness.
Delayed Internal Approvals	Undefined authority hierarchy	Publish a Delegation of Authority (DOA) and integrate digital approval workflow.
Lost Bid Learning Gaps	No structured review of bid losses	Conduct Monthly Post-Bid Review Meetings and capture lessons into CRM knowledge base.
Pipeline Inflation	Inclusion of unverified or speculative leads	Enforce CRM Audit and Validation, ensuring every lead has supporting documentation.
Scope Creep During Bidding	Inconsistent revision tracking	Introduce Revision Control Logs for all RFQs and scope changes.
Overlapping Responsibilities	Undefined ownership between Sales & Estimation	Maintain a RACI Matrix to clarify who decides, approves, and informs.

Leadership Reflection: *Challenges do not make sales systems weaker. They show where discipline is lacking. When every problem is logged as an improvement record in CRM, the business stops responding and starts improving.*

11. Things I've Learned from the field

Discipline is tested when there are live bids and client interactions, which is when real learning happens. These field experiences highlight how little mistakes or clear communication may completely impact the course of an organization.

Case 5: The Cost of Making Assumptions

A contractor who fixes valves rushed to send in a quote during a refinery turnaround. The RFQ said "alloy steel components," which the team though meant ordinary grades. After the award the client made it clear that they needed an exotic alloy, which increased the cost of buying it. The project was finished, but the final margin reduced by 22%, which was a costly lesson in the cost of making assumptions.

> *Leadership takeaway: Assumptions are hidden costs. Every mistake you make today will be comes an expense tomorrow.*

Case 6: The Power of Making Things Clear

A fabrication crew found that the designs and the equipment list didn't match up in a complicated piping operation. They asked for official explanation instead of making assumptions, and they attached side-by-side mark-ups with clear questions in a systematic way. The client's technical team was impressed by how professional and open the company was. There was no bargaining for the proposal, and the company got a formal letter of thanks for "exceptional technical diligence."

> *Leadership takeaway: Being clear develops confidence, and confidence speeds up closing. In sales, integrity communicated via inquiries frequently wins faster than promises expressed through assumptions.*

12. Precision Pointers: Best Practices for Sales Governance

Sales governance is the art of turning possibilities into performance that can be counted on. The principles below assist turn sales from something you do when you have to into a planned, data-driven activity.

Precision Pointers

- Use every lead as data: keep track of, assess, and update each opportunity. Missing data means missing out on an opportunity.

- Don't just use the 5-stage funnel as a formality. Use it as a discipline check. Every stage should ensure scope, risk and readiness.

- Make Go/No-Go decisions based on facts and capacity, not hope: Speculations is having faith without being able to do something.

- Connect operations and finance to CRM: A connected system makes sure that the accuracy of forecasts, the amount of effort, and the flow of cash are all in sync.

- Go over lost bids in a systematic way: Each lost should teach you something that helps you better your templates, price logic, or qualifying filters.

- Celebrate qualified rejections: Saying no to work that doesn't fit with your goals is a sign of mature organization, not a loss of money.

- Check Sales Metrics Every Month: Long before the balance sheet, trends in DSO, ratios, and funnel conversion rates show how well a process is working long before the balance sheet does.

- Keep a record of every decision trail: Being open and honest with clients and team members develops trust.

> **Leadership Reflection**: Sales governance makes change a deliberate choice. The ability to decide wisely is both the foundation and the first sign of a truly process-driven culture.

13. Summary: Lead Discipline as the Basis of Reliability

Sales and opportunity management are what determine, how reliably a business keeps its commitments, it is the first Phase in the AG Business Flow Framework, where systematic lead handling sets the pace for estimating, carrying out, and paying for things.

Every disciplined quote make predictions more accurate. Every valid denial keeps profits safe. And every decision that is written down makes the organization's memory stronger.

Sales and opportunity management define how reliably an organisation promises and delivers. It forms **Phase 1** of AG **Business Flow Framework**, where structured lead handling sets the rhythm for estimation, execution, and finance.

Every disciplined quotation improves forecasting accuracy. Every qualified rejection protects profitability. And every documented decision strengthens organisational memory.

Executive Summary:

The first sign of reliability is sales discipline. Every choice to pursue or decline affects the organization's integrity long before a contract is signed.

- **Discipline is credibility:** Every well-organized lead makes clients confidence and your team trust.
- **Why qualification is strategy:** Selective pursuit
- structured lead builds client confidence and internal trust.

- **Qualification is Strategy:** Selective pursuit protects profits more than any discount ever will.

- **Control is visibility:** When CRM governance translates data into direction, leaders shift from reacting to predicting.

- **Feedback is money:** Each lost bid teaches you something that helps you win the next one without spending money. Integrity is a legacy: Only promise what you can deliver exactly, because credibility grows quicker than income.

Chapter 3: Estimation & Proposal Management

AG Business Flow Framework™

"Precision builds trust before execution begins."

1. Reframing Estimation: From Math to Confidence

In the AG Business Flow Framework, **Phase 2: Estimation Precision** defines an organisation's credibility long before the first activity begins.

Estimation is often mistaken for a mathematical exercise. In truth, it is the language of confidence. It is a disciplined translation of uncertainty into dependable numbers. A precise estimate tells both clients and leadership that the company does more than calculate cost, it understands cause.

Every number carries a story:

- of scope clarity
- of productivity assumptions
- of vendor reliability
- of historical learning

When these stories align, numbers gain authority. That is why a strong estimator is not a calculator but a risk communicator. Someone who converts technical ambiguity into managerial foresight.

Clients, management, and engineers all seek one thing before execution: trust in the estimate. Because trust in the estimate is trust in the organisation's discipline.

AG Estimation Philosophy

"We not only understand your scope, we understand ourselves."

2. Purpose of Estimation Precision

Estimation precision does what no calculator ever can. It transforms uncertainty into organisational confidence.

- **Transforms Ambiguity into Structure:** Converts undefined scope into measurable tasks, quantifies risk, and establishes logical sequence. Precision replaces guesswork with clarity and accountability.

- **Builds Cross-Functional Alignment:** Ensures that sales, engineering, procurement, finance, and operations speak the same cost language. When everyone interprets data through a shared baseline, coordination replaces assumption.

- **Protects Credibility:** A disciplined estimator protects reputation by preventing over-promising in pursuit and under-delivering in execution. Estimation precision is not about predicting the future perfectly. It is about preparing for it responsibly.

Leadership Reflection: Precision is not the absence of error. It is the control of variability through method, validation, and feedback.

3. Estimate Classification Levels

In professional project management practice, estimates are classified according to the definition level of scope, data maturity, and expected accuracy range. These classification levels help organisations align effort, confidence, and decision risk at each stage of project development.

In simple terms:

- **Class 5** represents early conceptual or feasibility estimates, where information is minimal and accuracy is broad.
- **Class 4** refines the concept using preliminary engineering inputs and parametric or analogous data.
- **Class 3** is typically used for budget or bid preparation, supported by partial quantities and vendor inputs.
- **Class 2** serves as the tender or control baseline, developed from detailed engineering and verified quotations.
- **Class 1** provides the definitive estimate, prepared from fully defined design and execution data, offering the highest level of confidence for final approval and contracting.

Interpretation Example

A budgetary estimate of 10 million dollars prepared at an intermediate definition level, roughly equivalent to a Class 3 estimate, may carry an accuracy range of ±25%. This means the likely final cost could fall between 7.5 million dollars and 12.5 million dollars. The leadership decision lies in assessing whether that level of uncertainty is acceptable for the project's current stage and overall risk appetite.

> *Leadership Insight: The value of estimate classification lies not in the numbers themselves but in the discipline it demands. It defines how much is known, how much is assumed, and how confidently the organisation can act.*

4. The Accuracy vs Effort Curve

Every estimate begins as a guess and matures into a guarantee. The journey between the two is shaped by definition and discipline, by how much information is known and how methodically it is processed.

Accuracy improves as project definition deepens, but each improvement demands significantly more effort. Early estimates can be prepared within hour, while definitive ones may require weeks of engineering input, supplier quotation, and cross-functional validation.

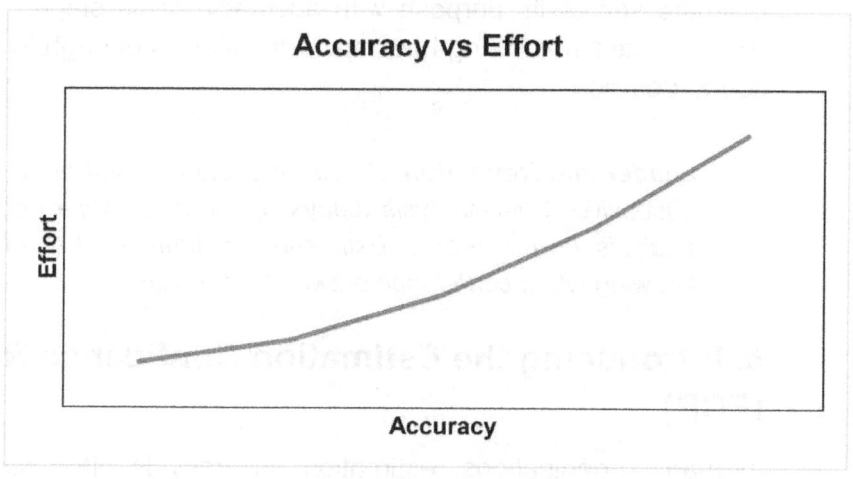

Figure 2 - Accuracy vs Effort

Interpretation

- The greatest improvement in accuracy occurs between **Class 5** and **Class 3**, when conceptual data evolves into measurable quantities and structured costing.
- Beyond **Class,** further refinement consumes significant resources but yields diminishing returns. This point marks the classic accuracy-effort inflection.

- A mature organisation learns to choose the right estimation class for the right decision. The goal is not perfect numbers, but precision that fits the purpose.

Illustrative Example:

A client may request a Class 3 estimate (±25%) to gain an initial understanding of project cost while preparing the annual budget. At this stage, the estimate relies on conceptual scope, preliminary quantities, and benchmark data to define investment direction. Once the project moves into detailed design and tendering, Class 1 estimation (±10%) is developed based on engineered drawings, verified material take-offs, and confirmed vendor quotations. Each estimate serves its purpose with accuracy for its stage. The rue discipline lies in knowing how much definition is enough to make a sound decision.

> *Leadership Reflection: Precision should be sufficient, not obsessive. Over-analysis delays opportunity, while under-analysis invites regret. Estimation maturity is the art of knowing when confidence outweighs curiosity.*

5. Introducing the Estimation Confidence Ratio (ECR)

In many organisations, estimation accuracy is often discussed through opinions rather than evidence. The **AG Business Flow Framework** changes this perception by introducing a measurable performance indicator called the **Estimation Confidence Ratio (ECR).**

Formula

ECR = $(1 - ((\text{Estimated Cost} - \text{Actual Cost}) / \text{Actual Cost})) \times 100$

ECR measures how closely the estimated cost aligns with the actual outcome. It is not intended to punish deviation but to assess learning precision and process discipline.

Interpretation

ECR Range	Meaning	Organizational Maturity Signal
95–100 %	Highly confident	Predictive and data-driven
85–94 %	Controlled	Consistent process feedback
70–84 %	Reactive	Weak scope clarity or limited learning
< 70 %	Unreliable	People-dependent estimation culture

An organisation that maintains an **ECR of 90% or higher** across multiple projects demonstrates predictive maturity. It reflects the capability to estimate with confidence because its process, data, and feedback systems are properly aligned.

Example

A service company estimated a shutdown job at **4.8 million USD**, and the actual cost closed at **5.0 million USD.**

ECR = (1 − (4.8 − 5.0) / 5.0) × 100 = 96%

An ECR of 96% signals a highly reliable estimation process. It is not perfect, but it is confident and controlled. By comparison, another project with and ECR of 75% reveals not failure but a learning opportunity. The gap often lies in unverified assumptions, outdated cost inputs, or missing productivity feedback from operations. When estimation and execution team share performance data consistently, the ECR becomes more than a number. It becomes a reflection of how effectively experience is being recycled into future precision.

> *Leadership Reflection: ECR is the mirror of estimation discipline. It tells leaders not what went wrong, but how well the system learns to be right the next time.*

26

When tracked consistently, ECR evolves into an organisational KPI that strengthens accountability, feedback, and continuous improvement. Teams stop defending their estimates and start refining them.

6. Estimation Approaches and Their Application

Different estimation approaches offer varying levels of confidence depending on how much information is available. Industry-recognised project management standards define several approaches, each suited to particular stage of scope definition and decision-making maturity.

Type	Accuracy (±)	When Used	Typical Basis
Analogous	15–30 %	Quick comparisons during early phases	Data from similar past projects
Parametric	5–20 %	Feasibility and budget planning	Statistical cost per unit
Bottom-Up	5–10 %	Tender and execution control	Detailed WBS and quantities
Three-Point (PERT)	Range-based	Complex or high-risk scope	Optimistic, Most Likely, Pessimistic

Integration Insight: Each Estimation Approach can serve a corresponding Estimate Class:

- Conceptual corresponds to Analogous (Class 5 to 4)
- Budgetary corresponds to Parametric or Bottom-Up (Class 3)
- Control corresponds to Bottom-Up methods (Class 2 to 1)

In mature organisations, ECR data from completed projects feedback into both parametric and analogous models. This continuous loop of learning turns operational experience into measurable accuracy.

7. Cost Build-Up & Risk Allowance

Every reliable estimate is built like an engineered structure, supported by defined cost components and disciplined risk provisions. Cost built-up is not a spreadsheet exercise. It is a form of financial design that converts technical understanding into commercial confidence.

Direct Costs: The Tangible Core

Direct costs are the measurable elements directly linked to scope delivery:

- **Materials:** All consumables, components, and spare parts derived from BOMs or take-offs.

- **Labour:** Estimated man-hours multiplied by validated productivity norms, adjusted for learning curve and shift factors.

- **Equipment:** Owned or hired machinery, including setup, operation, and standby costs.

- **Subcontracts:** Specialist works such as thrust boring, insulation, or machining, priced through vendor quotations.

  Leadership Note: Direct costs define execution reality. Every inaccuracy here multiplies downstream. Validation through historical data and feedback loops ensures repeatable precision.

Indirect Costs: The Hidden Enablers

Indirect costs sustain the project but do not directly produce the deliverable. They include:

- **Supervision & QA/QC:** Site management, inspectors, planners, and document controllers.

- **Facilities:** Site offices, utilities, tools, PPE, and temporary infrastructure.

- **Administration & Logistics:** Mobilization, accommodation, local transport, and IT connectivity.

Indirect costs are often underestimated because they appear intangible, yet they determine whether a project runs smoothly or struggles under strain. Benchmarking and cost-code segregation are key to maintaining visibility.

Risk Allowance: Managing the Known-Unknowns

Even the best estimates face uncertainties such as vendor delays, weather interruptions, or minor scope clarifications. A **Risk Allowance** typically 1–3% is applied for such known-unknowns, risks that can be listed, quantified, and mitigated. Each allowance should be tied to a corresponding entry in the **Project Risk Register** so it can be tracked, released, or reallocated as conditions evolve.

> **Best Practice**: Risk allowances are not permanent buffers. They are controlled provisions governed by review rules and risk accountability.

Contingency: Guarding Against the Unknown-Unknowns

Contingency covers what experience cannot predict, such as design changes, unforeseen ground conditions, or supply-chain disruptions. Typical ranges are guided by estimation class:

- **Class 5–4:** 10–15%
- **Class 3:** 5–10%
- **Class 2–1:** 3–5%

Contingency is not a sign of weak estimation. It is a sign of mature foresight. It must be visible in the estimate summary, approved by management, and governed by **release rules** linked to project milestones. Hidden contingencies erode trust, visible ones reinforce credibility.

Profit / Mark-Up: Balancing Reward and Risk

Profit is not a random uplift. It is a calibrated reflection of risk, competition, and capability. Market maturity demands balance:

- **High Risk / Tight Schedule:** Higher mark-up to compensate for uncertainty.
- **Repeat or Framework Jobs:** Lower mark-up justified by efficiency and trust.
- **Strategic Entry Projects:** Controlled margin for market positioning.

Leadership Insight: Profit must be earned through predictability, not recovered through change orders. In process-driven organization, mark-up reflects value created, not luck recovered.

Integrating the Build-Up

A mature estimate connects all layers of cost components including direct, indirect, risk, contingency, and profit into a transparent summary.

Component	Purpose	Control Mechanism
Direct Costs	Define scope execution value	Verified take-offs & norms
Indirect Costs	Sustain delivery environment	Benchmarked cost codes
Risk Allowance	Quantify controllable uncertainties	Risk Register tracking
Contingency	Protect against unforeseeable factors	Release by approval stage
Profit / Mark-Up	Reward for capability and exposure	Management policy review

> ***Cultural Message:*** *Treat contingency as a visible reserve with release discipline, not as hidden padding. Transparency in cost build-up converts financial caution into client confidence. When every percentage is justified and traceable, estimation becomes not only accurate but honourable.*

8. Case Study: The Bid That Missed the Mark

Background

A mid-sized fabrication company bid aggressively for a process skid package against larger EPC competitors. The estimator, under pressure to meet the submission deadline, assumed that welding could be handled entirely in-house and that vendor lead times would align with plan. To appear competitive, the risk allowance was minimized and all contingencies were removed. The price looked sharp, and the contract was awarded.

Outcome

Victory was short-lived. Once execution began, the company discovered that the specialized fittings required longer lead times than expected. Vendor delays forced the use of air freight, emergency subcontracting, and round-the-clock rework to recover schedule. The project closed **27%** over the estimated cost, resulting in an **ECR of 73%**, a clear indicator of lost estimation discipline.

The win that was celebrated in the bid room became a post-mortem in the boardroom.

Diagnosis

Missed Control Point	Impact
No clarification of vendor delivery variance	Schedule slippage and air freight cost

Missed Control Point	Impact
Risk allowance removed "to be competitive"	Zero flexibility during crisis
Review cycle compressed to 48 hours	Incomplete cross-functional validation
No post-bid peer review	Repeated assumptions in future bids

The team did not fail in mathematics. They failed in **method**. Their numbers were correct, but their process was incomplete.

> **Leadership Reflection:** *Competitiveness without precision is a race to regret. True leaders win bids not by cutting risk but by calculating it transparently. The most expensive project is often the one priced too low to deliver with honour.*

9. Estimation Review Cycle Checklist

A strong estimation process is not only about accuracy, it's about **assurance.** Each review stage converts a technical calculation into an organizational commitment. When executed correctly, the review cycle becomes the control mechanism that transforms **numbers into trust.**

Purpose of the Review Cycle

Every estimate represents a financial promise to both the client and the company. Before that promise is released, it must pass through a structured verification chain that ensures clarity, consistency, and credibility. This is the foundation of **Phase 2, Estimation Precision** within the AG Business Flow Framework™.

Estimation Review Stages

Stage	Focus Area	Leadership Questions
Self-Check	Completeness and documentation	Have all scope items been included? Are drawings at the latest revision? Are key assumptions clearly logged?
Peer Review	Cross-disciplinary validation	Are productivity norms realistic? Are inter-discipline dependencies covered? Is the risk register updated and quantified?
Commercial Review	Financial accuracy and compliance	Are vendor quotes valid and comparable? Have escalation factors and exchange rates been applied? Are margins aligned with corporate policy?
Management Review	Strategic and capacity alignment	Does the pricing reflect the organization's delivery capacity? Is the declared Estimate Class appropriate for this bid stage? Are there potential contractual exposures?
Archival & Feedback	Knowledge retention and improvement	Has the estimate, along with its ECR target, been logged in the project database? Are deviations from similar past jobs analysed for future learning?

Best Practice Guidelines

- **Set Review Timelines Early:** Schedule all review checkpoints before submission to prevent last-minute compression.
- **Maintain Traceability:** Each review comment should be logged, acted upon, and acknowledged.
- **Quantify Review Impact:** Measure how many value or risk changes were identified at each stage. This demonstrates process ROI, the return on intelligence, not just investment.

- **Feed Forward, Not Just Back:** Post-project review findings must update future estimating norms, not just archives.

Leadership Insight: A reviewed estimate is not paperwork, it is an audited promise. Review discipline transforms estimation from a cost exercise into a culture of foresight. The true strength of an organization's numbers lies not in who prepared them, but in how many eyes refined them before release.

10. Digital Enablement and ECR Tracking

Modern estimation precision no longer depends solely on expert judgment. It depends on digital discipline. Technology doesn't replace estimators, it enhances their accuracy, memory, and speed. In a mature organization, every estimate is backed by systems that capture, validate, and continuously improve data integrity.

Central Rate Database and Revision Logs

The backbone of digital estimation is a centralised rate library, a single source of truth for materials, labour norms, equipment, and overheads. Each revision is time-stamped and traceable. When estimators work from standardised rates, the organisation eliminates one of the most common causes of error, inconsistency. Revision logs also serve as audit trails, reinforcing transparency and accountability.

Leadership Note: Consistency in cost data builds credibility faster than any low price can.

ERP Integration for Cost Traceability

Integration with **Enterprise Resource Planning (ERP)** systems ensures that estimated costs, purchase orders, and actual expenditures speak the same language. This linkage allows:

- Real-time variance tracking between planned and actual costs.
- Instant access to project-level margins and financial exposure.
- Direct ECR feedback once projects close.

ERP integration transforms estimation into the first step of **financial intelligence**, not a standalone department.

3D/5D Take-offs Linked to the WBS

By connecting 3D models for geometry and 5D modules for cost and schedule, estimators can extract quantities directly from engineering designs. Each Work Breakdown Structure (WBS) code links physical quantities to financial values, ensuring traceability from drawing to invoice. This reduces manual take-off errors, compresses estimation time, and aligns cost data with construction sequencing. The result is visual accuracy replacing assumption-driven calculations.

AI-Driven ECR Monitoring Across Projects

Artificial Intelligence brings learning at scale. By analysing historical estimates and actuals, AI models can detect cost anomalies, predict underestimation trends, and flag bias in specific disciplines or project types. When ECRs from past projects feed into AI systems, they generate predictive benchmarks that show how future estimates are likely to perform even before execution begins.

Example: The system identifies that piping jobs over 10,000 weld dia.-inch tend to underperform by 8% on average. The estimator adjusts productivity norms accordingly, improving accuracy proactively.

Barcode Feedback to Validate Man-Hour Norms

On-site barcode scanning connects reality back to the estimate. When technicians log their job start and completion using barcode or mobile systems, man-hour data flows directly into dashboards.

This real-time productivity feedback helps refine future labour norms, aligning estimation models with actual field performance.

Outcome: The estimation sheet becomes a live feedback loop, not a static document.

ECR Dashboards: From Experience to Evidence

All these systems converge in **ECR Dashboards,** visual platforms that display:

- Project-wise ECR trends
- Discipline accuracy heat maps
- Estimator performance consistency
- Variance causes such as scope, procurement, productivity, or pricing

These dashboards turn organisational memory into measurable foresight. Leaders no longer ask, "How accurate were we?" They now ask, "Where will our next variance come from, and how can we prevent it?"

> **Leadership Reflection:** *Digital tools do not build precision, they reveal it. Technology ensures that every lesson learned is captured, verified, and shared. When experience becomes evidence, estimation evolves from calculation to prediction, and from prediction to confidence.*

11. Leadership Commentary: Precision as Culture

> *"Precision is not about decimal points, it is about discipline repeated daily"*
>
> *AG Business Flow Framework*

Precision in estimation is not a mathematical virtue, it is a cultural one. It reflects how seriously a company values preparation, clarity, and accountability. Numbers may be calculated by a few, but their accuracy represents the mindset of all.

In mature organisations, estimation is treated as a leadership behaviour, not merely a departmental function. Leaders set the tone by defining what precision means, not just in figures but in expectations, reviews, and learning habits.

Guidelines for Leaders

- **Set ECR Targets and Review Them Quarterly:** Establish Estimation Confidence Ratio (ECR) benchmarks for each project type. Discuss them in management meetings as indicators of organisational foresight, not just estimation skill. Celebrate when ECR trends improve. It proves that your systems are learning.

- **Invest in Data Quality before Software:** Digital tools amplify whatever culture they serve. If the data is unreliable, technology will only multiply the confusion. Build clean rate libraries, unified cost codes, and verified productivity norms before expanding systems.

- **Recognize Estimators Who Ask the Right Questions, Not Just Deliver Fast:** Speed is visible, curiosity is invaluable. Reward those who challenge assumptions, clarify uncertainties, and document their reasoning. They are the architects of accuracy.

- **Communicate That Estimate Accuracy Defines Organizational Reliability:** When leadership ties estimation precision to company reputation, accountability spreads across departments. Everyone understands that accuracy is not just technical, it is ethical.

- **Protect the Review Cycle from Shortcuts Driven by Urgency.** The pressure to submit faster must never outweigh the discipline to submit correctly. A missed day in review can cost months in rework. Make "review completeness" a non-negotiable checkpoint before every submission.

Leadership Reflection: Precision is culture before it becomes competence. When leaders model patience, verification, and clarity, teams stop rushing for closure and start working for confidence. The moment an organisation respects accuracy as a shared responsibility, estimation transforms from a department's task into a company's character.

12. Ethics and Professional Integrity

Estimation defines not only what a company knows but also who it is. Every number issued carries a moral weight, as it represents the organisation's honesty, fairness, and accountability. That is why estimation excellence cannot exist without ethical discipline. A precise figure without integrity is simply a well-calculated error.

Ethical Principles of Estimation

- **Transparency in Assumptions and Exclusions:** Every assumption, whether related to material source, productivity rate, or scope limitation, must be clearly declared. Hidden exclusions destroy credibility faster than technical mistakes. Transparency ensures that the client, management, and operations team all begin from the same version of truth.

- **Confidentiality and Respect for Information:** Estimators often handle sensitive vendor quotes, proprietary process data, and client budgets. Guarding this information is not optional, it is a professional obligation. Breaches of confidentiality not only violate trust but also compromise competitive fairness.

- **Honesty in Numbers:** Never adjust figures to meet management expectations or to "win" a bid. Manipulated optimism is disguised risk. Leadership must encourage estimators to present reality, even when it is uncomfortable, because credibility today prevents crisis tomorrow.

- **Commitment to Fair Competition.** Uphold anti-bribery and anti-collusion standards in all dealings. Professional reputation, once damaged, cannot be rebuilt with spreadsheets. True competitiveness is built on clarity, capability, and ethical confidence.

- **Accountability in Representation.** When an estimator signs off on a proposal, it represents not only a cost but a commitment. That signature is a pledge of accuracy, professionalism, and good faith.

Leadership Reflection: Precision without ethics is still an error. Ethics is the invisible quality control of every estimate. It ensures that truth and trust share the same number. In a world where prices can be copied, only integrity cannot be imitated.

13. Transition to Phase 3: Order Confirmation & Handover

When an estimate wins a contract, its true value is tested in how well it transfers to execution. A structured handover must include the approved estimate, risk register, and clarification trail.

"The first proof of estimation precision is how accurately execution can follow it."

14. Lessons Learned

Estimation precision is more than a numerical exercise, it is organisational confidence made visible. Every estimate tells a story about how clearly a company understands its scope, its risks, and its own discipline. The moment accuracy becomes repeatable, confidence becomes measurable.

- **Data Quality Drives Accuracy, Review Discipline Sustains It:** Good data builds strong numbers, but only consistent reviews keep them credible. Every unchecked assumption today becomes tomorrow's cost variance.

- **The ECR Is a Mirror of Maturity. Measure it and Act on It:** The Estimation Confidence Ratio (ECR) reflects not perfection but learning. Continuous tracking turns estimation into an intelligent feedback system that teaches the organisation how to improve itself.

- **Over-Aggressive Pricing Destroys Trust Faster Than It Wins Orders:** Short-term victories earned by undercutting accuracy lead to long-term credibility loss. Sustainable success is built on transparent logic, not tactical optimism.

- **Precision Requires Both Tools and Temperament:** Software delivers speed, mindset delivers reliability. Estimators who combine analytical rigour with ethical clarity become the quiet architects of a company's reputation.

Leadership Reflection: Precision is not perfection, it is alignment with purpose. When accuracy becomes culture, every number speaks the truth of the organisation behind it.

15. Leadership Insight

"Data builds numbers, discipline builds trust."

AG Business Flow Framework

Numbers can be calculated by anyone, but discipline in estimation, that deliberate balance between speed and certainty, defines a company's credibility. Every formula can compute cost, but only culture can ensure confidence.

When discipline is repeated across bids, reviews, and feedback loops, precision becomes habit. And when precision becomes habit, trust becomes automatic within teams, with clients, and across leadership levels. True maturity in estimation is not the ability to predict the future perfectly, but the ability to be trusted even when the future changes.

Chapter 4: Order Confirmation & Handover

AG Business Flow Framework™

"Precision turns into performance when teams hand over clarity, not files."

1. From Precision to Performance

Every project that wins on paper must first earn its readiness in practice. The bridge between the bid and the build is Order Confirmation and Handover, the moment when technical precision meets execution reality.

In many companies, this moment decides whether a project will flow smoothly or struggle with rework and disputes. A seamless handover ensures that what was promised can truly be delivered on scope, on time, and on budget.

> **Leadership Reflection:** *A perfect bid without an aligned handover is a delayed project in disguise.*

2. The Purpose of Order Confirmation

A Purchase Order is the client's commitment, while confirmation is the company's confidence. It transforms an external promise into an internal authorisation, converting intent instruction.

Order confirmation is the moment when leadership says, "We agree to deliver, knowing exactly what we are accountable for." It ensures that the enthusiasm from the award is grounded in structure, alignment, and verified readiness.

Core Objectives

- **Validate Contractual Integrity:** Confirm that all technical and commercial terms in the client's Purchase Order precisely reflect the final approved proposal. This includes scope, exclusions, deliverables, payment milestones, and any negotiated variations. Small deviations at this stage often grow into large disputes later.

- **Identify Risks Before Start:** Early confirmation allows a structured review of delivery feasibility, logistics, and contractual obligations. It is easier to negotiate clarifications before work begins than to argue those after costs have been incurred.

- **Assign Ownership:** Each discipline, including sales, estimation, operations, procurement, and finance, receives formal ownership of its commitments. This marks the shift from individual effort to institutional responsibility and accountability.

- **Create Project Codes:** Order Confirmation (IOC) triggers the creation of project codes in the ERP system for cost, billing, and reporting. This ensures that all future expenses, purchase orders, and invoices trace back to one verifiable financial source of truth.

Leadership Reflection: Order confirmation transforms enthusiasm into executable structure. It is the organisational handshake between ambition and accountability, where precision in estimation becomes performance in execution.

3. Process Flow Snapshot

Every successful project begins with a disciplined confirmation flow, a sequence that translates a client's purchase order into an executable plan.

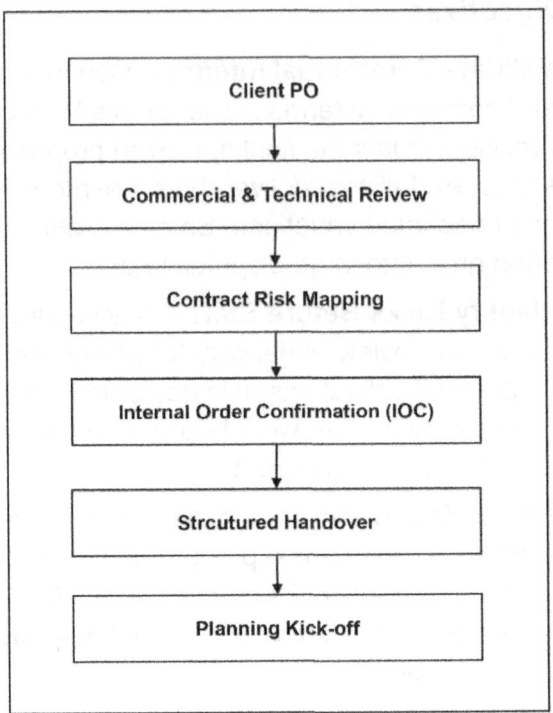

Figure 3 - Process Flow

Each arrow represents a control gate that validates one dimension of reliability across commercial, technical, contractual, organisational, and finally operational. This simple flow underpins the discipline that prevents downstream chaos and ensures that every promise moves through proof before action.

4. Commercial and Technical Review

The first safeguard against execution risk is alignment, confirming that what the client ordered is exactly what the company priced and can deliver.

Commercial Validation

Check	Focus	Control Action
Payment Termes	Milestones / Retention	Align with approved proposal or escalate for amendment.
Taxes / Duties	VAT, WHT	Verify compliance with current regulations.
Guarantees	Type & cost	Obtain management approval before commitment
Insurance	Coverage scope	Match project policy and client requirement.
Currency	FX risk	Hedge exposure or fix rate contractually.

Commercial validation protects **profitability** by ensuring financial terms mirror the approved bid. No hidden liabilities and no silent cost leaks.

Technical Validation

- Confirm latest drawings and specifications.
- Reconcile exclusions and assumptions from the proposal.
- Verify delivery feasibility against resource and vendor readiness.
- Prepare a Scope Clarification Note for formal record.

> **Leadership Reflection:** *Financial accuracy protects profit, and technical accuracy protects credibility. A contract signed without alignment is a dispute waiting to mature.*

5. Contract Review and Risk Mapping

Once validation is complete, the focus shifts from checking to foreseeing. A Contract Review Meeting brings together sales, estimation, operations, finance, procurement, and QA/QC. Its purpose is to expose hidden risks before they expose the company.

Risk Area	Example	Mitigation Action
Scope	Undefined interfaces	Clarify ownership before kick-off.
Schedule	Aggressive timeline	Re-sequence or phase execution.
Commercial	Milestones tied to client shutdowns	Renegotiate structure for cash-flow balance.
Legal	Penalty clauses	Legal vetting and management approval.
Technical	Single-vendor dependency	Qualify alternates or backup suppliers.

The outcome is a concise Risk Register, the project's early-warning radar. It defines not only what could go wrong but also who is responsible for preventing it.

> *Leadership Insight: When risk is identified early, it becomes cost. When found late, it becomes a crisis.*

6. Internal Order Confirmation (IOC)

After risks are mapped and terms validated, the organization formalizes its internal commitment through the Internal Order Confirmation. The IOC is more than approval, it is the company's internal contract.

IOC Includes

- Project and client details
- Approved budget and target margin
- Assigned project manager and team
- Start and completion dates
- Invoicing and payment milestones
- Linked estimate reference and risk register ID

Each IOC creates the official project codes in the ERP system for cost, billing, and progress control, ensuring that every future transaction traces back to a single financial source of truth.

> *Leadership Reflection: The IOC transforms agreement into accountability. It is not paperwork, it is the contract within the company, where precision becomes permission and enthusiasm becomes execution.*

7. Purpose of Handover

A disciplined handover ensures that every department begins from the same truth, not from assumptions, interpretations, or incomplete emails. It is the point where knowledge becomes accountability and documentation becomes direction.

In most project failures, the issue is rarely technical, it is translational. What was estimated is not what is executed. Handover removes that translation gap by transferring verified knowledge, not just files or drawings.

Core Purpose

- **Unify Understanding Across Functions:** he handover meeting aligns estimation, operations, procurement, QA/QC, finance, and planning around one shared scope. It ensures that what was promised to the client can be delivered by the team.

- **Convert Data into Action:** Drawings, cost codes, and risk registers are no longer references. They become operational control points. Ownership shifts from "who prepared" to "who performs."

- **Preserve the Line of Accountability:** Each document handed over is a traceable commitment. The team that estimated the project passes forward its logic, assumptions, and constraints, ensuring that execution starts informed, not improvising.

46

- **Protect Profitability and Schedule Integrity:** Clear handover eliminates double work, procurement delays, and scope misunderstandings, the silent killers of margin. A sixty-minute structured meeting can prevent months of cost leakage.

Leadership Reflection: Handover is not a meeting, it is a mindset. It marks the moment when estimation confidence turns into execution control, when knowledge stops being personal and becomes institutional. When every project begins from the same version of truth, performance stops depending on people and starts depending on process.

8. Handover Excellence Checklist

A flawless handover does not depend on memory, it depends on structure. This checklist ensures that every critical document, responsibility, and control point is verified before execution begins. It transforms information into instruction.

Deliverable	Responsible Dept.	Control Point
Final Quotation & Estimate	Estimation	Cost vs. Purchase Order verified
Contract / PO	Commercial	Revision and terms confirmed
Scope Clarification Note	Estimation	Reviewed and signed by Project Manager
Risk Register	Contracts / QA	Risks logged, owners assigned
Payment Schedule	Finance	Uploaded and tracked in ERP
Drawings / Specifications	Engineering	Latest revision issued and acknowledged
Procurement Plan	Procurement	Vendor list and lead times validated

Deliverable	Responsible Dept.	Control Point
QA/QC & HSE Plans	Quality	Approved method statements and inspection criteria
Budget & Cost Codes	Finance	Activated and linked to project ERP codes
Communication Matrix	Project Manager	Distributed across all stakeholders
Document Index	Document Control	Access and version verified

Each checked item represents a closed loop of accountability. Nothing proceeds until data, documents, and departments align.

> **Leadership Reflection:** *Checklists do not slow projects, they keep them standing. In aviation, every flight begins with a checklist. In project execution, every success begins with a handover. Discipline at this stage prevents confusion from becoming costly later.*

9. RACI Matrix: Who Does What and When

The RACI Matrix converts accountability from assumption into agreement. It defines exactly who is Responsible, Accountable, Consulted, and Informed at every stage of order confirmation and handover. This matrix eliminates duplication, protects timelines, and builds clarity across functions.

Activity	R	A	C	I
Receive PO & Acknowledge	Sales	Commercial Manager	Estimation	Project Manager
Commercial Review	Finance	Commercial Manager	Legal	Sales
Technical Validation	Estimation	Engineering Head	QA/QC	Project Manager

Activity	R	A	C	I
Contract Review Meeting	Project Manager	Operations Head	Finance, QA/QC, Procurement	General Manager
IOC Approval	Commercial	General Manager / Director	Finance, Planning	All Departments
Handover Meeting	Estimation	Project Manager	QA/QC, Procurement, Finance	Client
Kick-off Preparation	Project Manager	Operations Head	Planning, Engineering	Stakeholders

RACI Legend

- **R - Responsible:** Executes the activity.
- **A - Accountable:** Owns the outcome and approval.
- **C - Consulted:** Provides expert input.
- **I - Informed:** Receives updates after decisions.

> *Leadership Reflection: Responsibility is clarity in action, and accountability is clarity in ownership. The RACI Matrix does not assign blame, it assigns focus. When everyone knows their "R" and "A," leadership no longer manages people, it manages process.*

10. Case Insight: The Missed Crane

During a major shutdown, the estimation team prepared a competitive bid for mechanical works. To stay lean, they assumed that cranes and lifting equipment would be provided by the client, a common industry practice but never confirmed in writing.

Weeks later, when the site team mobilised, no cranes were available. The assumption that was never communicated became a two-week delay. Emergency rentals followed, invoices piled up, and the project closed with a negative margin despite flawless execution. The error was not technical, it was procedural. The handover meeting never captured the assumption.

The Turnaround

Months later, the same team executed a similar shutdown project. This time, they followed the newly implemented Handover Excellence Checklist. Under the item Scope Clarification Note, the question "Who provides lifting equipment?" was flagged. The client confirmed it was excluded from their scope. The estimator raised a formal variation before mobilisation, cost approved and schedule intact.

The job finished on time, within budget, and with full client satisfaction.

> **Leadership Reflection:** *Process discipline is the fastest form of progress. Every hour spent clarifying assumptions saves days of rework. In mature organisations, mistakes do not repeat, they evolve into checklists that protect the next success.*

11. Communication & Integration

Smooth execution begins with structured communication. A disciplined handover is not only about transferring documents, it is about aligning people. Every department should receive the same message, at the same time, in the same format. This is how coordination evolves from conversation into culture.

A formal handover communication acts as the organisation's heartbeat. It synchronises intent before activity begins.

Best Practice Guidance

- Use one standard subject line for all handover notices, as it ensures instant recognition across departments.
- Attach or link the latest approved estimate, risk register, and clarification note to prevent version confusion.

- Circulate at least forty-eight hours before the meeting to allow each department to prepare inputs.

- Log acknowledgements, either through read receipts or ERP confirmation, to close the communication loop.

Leadership Reflection: Consistent messaging transforms departmental coordination into organisational rhythm. When communication becomes predictable, collaboration becomes natural. In process-driven cultures, alignment is not requested, it is rehearsed.

12. Finance and ERP Linkage

Once the handover concludes, Finance becomes the anchor of control. All cost, purchase, and billing data are linked under one unified project code in the ERP system. From this moment onward, every financial transaction, from purchase requisition to final invoice, traces back to the same digital record of truth.

This connection converts documentation into discipline. Budgets, commitments, and expenditures are no longer scattered across spreadsheets or emails, they are synchronised under one source of financial reality.

Integration Flow

- **Project Code:** The approved Internal Order Confirmation (IOC) triggers code creation in the ERP system. All related cost centres, budget lines, and control accounts are assigned automatically.

- **Cost & Commitment Linkage:** Procurement, stores, and subcontract payments post directly against the project code, providing real-time budget versus actual visibility.

- **Billing & Cash Flow Mapping:** Finance aligns payment milestones and retention schedules with the ERP ledger, ensuring that billing follows contractual logic, not guesswork.

- **Reporting & Analysis:** Dashboards pull from live ERP data, showing project profitability, commitment status, and forecast cash flow in a single consolidated view.

Leadership Reflection: Integration is not technology, it is transparency. Systems do not build control, behaviour does. When every department records truth in the same system, accountability becomes automatic and decisions become data-driven.

13. Handover Excellence Box: Five Operational Truths

Every successful execution flow begins with a clear handover philosophy. These five operational truths form the foundation of disciplined project continuity. They remind teams that reliability is engineered through clarity, not urgency.

- **Clarity before Velocity:** Speed without understanding only accelerates confusion.
- **System over Memory:** People move on, but structured data keeps the organisation consistent.
- **One Version of Truth:** Shared information builds unity, while scattered facts breed confusion.
- **Collaboration over Hierarchy:** Real discipline grows from dialogue, not in distance.
- **Learning over Blame:** Every handover should teach the next one how to do it better.

Together, these principles define operational maturity. They are simple enough to apply daily, yet powerful enough to sustain an organization for decades.

Leadership Reflection: Process discipline begins in documents but lives in behaviour. When clarity leads every transition, the organisation compounds efficiency and trust over time.

14. From Commitment to Control

When the handover closes, planning begins. All confirmed inputs, including scope, cost, risk, and milestones, flow directly into the Project Execution Plan (PEP). The baton passes from those who promised to those who perform.

This is the heartbeat of the AG Business Flow Framework™. Precision in Phase 2 evolves into Performance in Phase 3 and now transitions into Control in Phase 4.

Clarity is the starting point of control, because what begins organised rarely ends chaotic.

15. Closing Reflection

The Order Confirmation and Handover phase safeguards the company's credibility before a single tool touches the field. It is not paperwork, it is process insurance. By handing over clarity instead of files, organisations prevent scope drift, billing disputes, and wasted effort.

When every function speaks a common language of ownership, reliability no longer depends on individuals, it becomes the company's character.

When knowledge is transferred with precision, execution begins with confidence. And when confidence is repeatable, excellence becomes culture.

Chapter 5: Project Planning and Execution

AG Business Flow Framework™

"Control is not monitoring, it is pre-emptive clarity."

1. Bridge from Phase 3

As Phase 3, Order Confirmation and Handover, delivered clarity of intent, Phase 4, Execution Control, turns that clarity into controlled motion. At this stage, leadership moves from documentation to direction, ensuring that every decision taken during planning performs flawlessly on the ground.

> *Insight:* Precision becomes power only when clarity meets discipline.

2. Philosophy of Execution Control

Planning without control is optimism, and control without planning is firefighting. Execution Control combines foresight, feedback, and follow-through. It is not about watching the project unfold, it is about shaping outcomes before they occur.

In the AG Business Flow Framework, control is the phase where leadership transforms plans into predictability. At this stage, numbers, people, and processes converge to ensure that what was promised is delivered, not through pressure but through preparedness.

Dimensions of Control

Dimension	Meaning	Leadership Outcome
Predictive	Forecast outcomes using real-time data, trends, and leading indicators.	Reduces uncertainty before it becomes delay.
Preventive	Build safeguards and buffers before risks mature.	Avoids crisis through readiness.
Pre-emptive	Act on weak signals early, schedule drift, manpower gaps, material slippage.	Creates stability through anticipation.

Predictive Control answers the question: What's likely to happen next?

Preventive Control asks: What must we do now to stop it from going wrong?

Pre-emptive Control ensures: We never repeat the same mistake twice.

> *Lesson for Leaders: Control is leadership in advance, not supervision in delay. True control is invisible. It is the calm you see when everyone else expected chaos.*

3. Framework of Execution Control

Execution Control is the operational rhythm of discipline, the sequence through which planning transforms into predictable performance. Each stage builds on the last, creating a continuous chain of alignment, measurement, and learning. When followed systematically, this framework prevents reactive firefighting and replaces it with proactive leadership.

Execution Control Framework

Stage	Focus Area	Deliverables / Control Point	Leadership Intent
Kick-off & RACI	Define roles, responsibilities, and escalation paths.	Approved RACI matrix, communication hierarchy.	Ensures clarity before activity begins.
WBS & Scope Structuring	Break the project into measurable work packages and align cost codes.	Approved WBS and linked control codes.	Converts complexity into traceable structure.
Resource Readiness	Validate manpower, tools, and equipment against schedule.	Crew histogram, equipment mobilization plan.	Prevents idle time and early slippage.
Scheduling & CPA	Build a master schedule with dependencies and milestones.	Critical Path Analysis (CPA) and baseline schedule.	Makes time visible, enabling control by foresight.
Risk & HSE Integration	Embed risk register and safety controls into daily planning.	Updated risk log, permit-to-work matrix.	Converts safety from compliance to culture.
Execution & Variance Control	Monitor performance using earned value metrics (SPI/CPI).	Weekly progress and look-ahead reports.	Detects deviations early, enabling pre-emptive action.
Completion Gates	Validate readiness before billing or demobilization.	Completion checklist, QA/QC clearance, client sign-off.	Ensures deliverables equal documentation.

Stage	Focus Area	Deliverables / Control Point	Leadership Intent
Review & Feedback	Capture performance insights for future estimates.	Lessons Learned Report, ECR update.	Converts experience into enterprise intelligence.

Each stage represents one discipline of control, and skipping any stage introduces uncertainty downstream. Together, they form a feedback loop that connects estimation in Phase 2 to performance in Phase 4, closing the gap between plan and proof.

> *Leadership Reflection: Control is not achieved through oversight, it is engineered through sequence. When every stage is respected as a control gate, projects do not just finish, they finish with foresight.*

4. Kick-off and Responsibility Alignment

The kick-off meeting is where a signed contract becomes synchronised accountability. It converts the enthusiasm of winning a project into a structured plan for execution. At this stage, clarity of ownership is everything, because unclear responsibility is the most expensive risk an organisation can carry.

Each department formally reviews and signs the RACI Matrix, ensuring that everyone knows who acts, who approves, who supports, and who stays informed. This ritual turns coordination into commitment.

Sample RACI Snapshot

Activity	Responsible (R)	Accountable (A)	Consulted (C)	Informed (I)
Drawing Review	Design Engineer	Project Manager	QA/QC	Client

Activity	Responsible (R)	Accountable (A)	Consulted (C)	Informed (I)
Procurement	Buyer	Project Manager	Stores	Finance
Fabrication	Shop In-Charge	Operations Manager	QA/QC	Safety

The RACI Matrix does more than assign tasks, it defines the flow of authority and support. It also creates escalation clarity. When issues arise, the decision path is already mapped, preventing confusion and delays.

5. Scope Breakdown & Work Breakdown Structure (WBS)

A Work Breakdown Structure (WBS) is the skeleton of Execution Control. It breaks complexity into control points and transforms scope into measurable components. Without a WBS, a project is a collection of activities. With it, the project becomes a system of accountability.

A well-built WBS allows every department to speak the same operational language, linking planning, costing, scheduling, quality, and reporting through one framework of codes and ownership.

Purpose in Control

- Creates a common language for schedule, cost, QA/QC, and reporting.
- Enables measurable tracking of scope, progress, and responsibility.
- Connects planning data directly with ERP, scheduling tools, and field feedback
- Provides a traceable backbone for earned value (SPI/CPI) and performance dashboards.

WBS Structure

Level	Description	Example
1	Project	Valve Overhauling - 2025 Shutdown
2	Major Phase	Mobilization, Machining, Testing
3	Activity	"Dismantle 10 Valves," "Hydrotest Batch 1"
4	Task	Tag Valve #001–010 = 1 Unit

Each element has a unique code, an assigned owner, planned hours, and Completion Gate criteria, ensuring that progress is not only visible but verifiable.

Sample WBS Control Table

WBS Code	Phase	Deliverable	Gate Criteria
2.0	Dismantling	100 Valves Tagged	QC Tag List Signed
3.0	Machining	Seat Refacing	Inspection Report Approved
4.0	Assembly	Reassemble Valves	Hydrotest Passed
5.0	Painting	Final Coat	Paint Log Filed
6.0	Documentation & Demobilization	QA Pack	Client Release Certificate

Digital Linkage

Each WBS code is digitally connected across platforms:

Schedule → ERP → Barcode → QA Cloud

This chain of integration ensures that every unit of work is traceable from field activity to financial posting, from inspection status to billing readiness. It allows leadership to monitor progress, cost, and quality through a single version of truth.

> **Leadership Lesson:** *A strong WBS is not paperwork, it is navigation. It tells every engineer where they are, every planner what comes next, and every leader how close they are to control.*

6. Resource & Material Readiness

Control begins with readiness, because execution discipline is impossible without the right people, tools, and materials in place. Before a single task starts, leaders must confirm that resources are not just planned, they are prepared.

Resource Readiness Index

Resource Readiness Index (RRI) = (Available / Planned) × 100

A healthy readiness level is 95% or higher before project start. Anything below this threshold signals risk, delayed mobilisation, idle teams, or missed opportunities.

Control demands the right resources, at the right place, at the right time.

Manpower Readiness

Effective execution begins with readiness, not reaction. A disciplined approach to manpower preparation ensures that every resource arrives at the right time, with the right skill, and for the right task.

Before mobilization, leadership must verify readiness across skill, schedule, and documentation.

Checklist for manpower readiness

- Maintain a skill matrix for each crew category such as fitters, welders, inspectors, and supervisors.

- Cross-check mobilization dates against the schedule's first activity.
- Include training records, certifications, and visa or ID readiness in the mobilization checklist.
- Update availability of manpower versus plan weekly through ERP or timesheet dashboards.

If people arrive before plans, they wait. If plans arrive before people, time is lost. Control aligns both, ensuring that readiness becomes rhythm.

Equipment Readiness

Operational control begins with reliable equipment. Planned availability and preventive care ensure that machinery supports progress rather than interrupts it. Before execution starts, every major asset must be validated for performance, backup, and integration with the schedule.

Checklist for Equipment Readiness

- Target equipment uptime of 95% or higher, verified through preventive maintenance logs.
- Maintain a standby ratio for critical equipment such as cranes, generators, or welding machines.
- Integrate equipment allocation with the WBS and schedule to ensure that each activity has guaranteed support.

Material Readiness

Material readiness is the foundation of uninterrupted execution. Predictable flow depends on early identification, disciplined tracking, and clear visibility of every critical item. Leadership ensures that what is planned on paper is available in reality before work begins.

Checklist for material readiness

- Identify long-lead items such as valves, forgings, and exotic materials early, and link procurement milestones to the project schedule.

- Monitor each item through a Material Requisition (MR), Purchase Order (PO), Delivery, Inspection, and Issue tracking chain.

- Classify materials as critical-path dependent to ensure visibility during progress reviews.

Readiness is not inventory, it is assurance that work can start without waiting.

> *Leadership Reflection: Control is not what happens during execution, it is what is prevented before it begins. Every hour invested in readiness saves days of recovery. When teams start with 95% readiness, projects do not accelerate, they stabilise, and stability is the foundation of control.*

7. Scheduling and Critical Path Control

Scheduling is time visualised as discipline. A schedule is not a calendar of tasks, it is a forecast of accountability. It shows who owns time, how progress converts into performance, and where control must act before delay becomes visible.

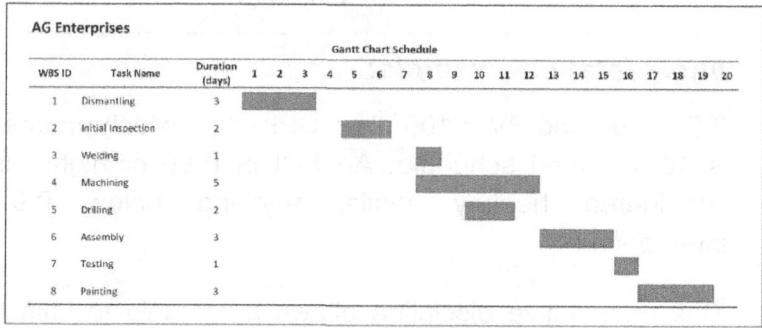

Figure 4 - Schdeule

Each block represents more than duration, it represents discipline in sequence.

Critical Path Control

Critical Path: Machining, Assembly, Testing, Painting

If machining slips by two days, the project end moves by two days. No other task can compensate for this. Leadership focus must therefore remain on critical path integrity, not on total activity count.

Control teams track and report critical path variance weekly, because every recovery day later costs exponentially more than prevention now.

> **Leadership Lesson:** *The Gantt chart is not a schedule, it is a forecast of consequences.*

Understanding Performance Formulas

Term	Meaning
EV (Earned Value)	The value of work actually completed.
PV (Planned Value)	The value that should have been completed by now.
SPI (Schedule Performance Index)	SPI = EV ÷ PV, Measures time efficiency.

Interpretation Example:

If EV = 90 and PV = 100, then SPI = 0.9, which means the project is 10% behind schedule. An SPI of 0.95 or higher is generally considered healthy, while anything below 0.9 demands intervention.

This quantitative discipline allows leadership to shift from status reporting to predictive correction.

Rolling Wave Planning

Projects evolve, and so must the schedule. Rolling Wave Planning means defining near-term tasks in full detail while keeping later phases broader and flexible. As time advances, details unfold progressively, preserving both clarity and agility.

Clarity builds precision, and agility sustains relevance. In Execution Control, a good plan is not one that never changes, but one that never surprises.

> *Leadership Reflection: Scheduling is not about predicting time, it is about protecting it. A disciplined leader reads the schedule not to monitor delay but to anticipate it. The power of control lies in foresight, not in follow-up.*

8. Mini Case: The Missing Permit Delay

During a refinery shutdown, the fabrication team waited five hours before work could begin because the hot work permit was still pending approval. Operations, safety, and maintenance teams each assumed the other had cleared it. The delay cost 18,000 US dollars in manpower, crane standby, and idle equipment within a single shift.

The post-review found no technical fault, only a missing checkpoint. To prevent recurrence, the team introduced a Permit Readiness Verification (PRV) gate in the daily control checklist. Before each shift begins, the supervisor confirms that all permits, including hot work, confined space, and isolation, are approved and logged.

Since implementing PRV, no permit-related delay has occurred across multiple shutdowns.

> *Leadership Lesson: Control is about sequencing readiness, not pushing speed. A mature system does not move faster, it moves smarter, ensuring every gate is cleared before motion begins.*

9. Completion Gates

In mature organisations, completion is not declared, it is verified. Each gate acts as a control checkpoint that confirms readiness before the project moves to the next stage. These gates ensure that deliverables are backed by documentation, quality, and commercial closure, converting operational progress into financial confidence.

Completion Gate Framework

Gate	Verified By	Criteria
G1 – Material Gate	Procurement	All purchase orders closed, materials delivered and inspected.
G2 – QA/QC Gate	QA/QC Engineer	Inspection & Test Plans (ITPs) approved, calibration and NCRs cleared.
G3 – Work Gate	Project Manager	Physical completion achieved, punch list items resolved.
G4 – Billing Gate	Finance	Service Entry Sheet (SES) prepared, client sign-off and invoice package ready.

Each gate converts progress into proof, ensuring that no step advances without validation. By embedding these checkpoints in both planning and reporting systems such as ERP or project dashboards, leadership maintains control without micromanagement.

> *Leadership Reflection: These gates turn handover into confidence, not debate. Control is not about questioning performance, it is about confirming readiness. When every milestone passes through evidence, reliability becomes measurable and disputes disappear.*

10. Quality, HSE and Compliance

Execution Control is not complete until it protects two things:

- The integrity of the work (Quality)
- The continuity of operations (Safety)

Compliance is the bridge between them. It translates standards into measurable behaviour. Together, these three elements ensure that performance is sustainable, not situational.

Quality: Conformance Creates Credibility

Quality begins long before inspection, it starts with planning. Every activity must trace back to an approved Inspection and Test Plan (ITP) that defines what will be inspected, when it will be done, and by whom.

Control Components

- **ITP Adherence:** 100% of completed work must have corresponding ITP records.
- **Calibration Integrity:** All instruments verified before use, with automated alerts for due dates.
- **Non-Conformance Tracking:** Each NCR logged, analysed, and closed with documented corrective action.
- **Digital QA Index:** Percentage of ITP checkpoints passed without rework, target 95% or higher.

Why it matters: Quality failures do not only create rework, they destroy trust. A single unverified weld or unrecorded test can wipe out weeks of progress.

Quality is not inspection at the end. it is verification at every step.

HSE: Safety is the Engine of Continuity

Safety programmes prevent downtime and protect competence. No system can claim control while allowing unsafe shortcuts.

Core Mechanisms

- **Permit-to-Work (PTW):** While PTQ are typically issued and controlled by the client, internal systems can maintain a digital log to track status, reference permit numbers, and ensure all internal readiness checks are complete before a permit is requested. This creates alignment without breaching client-controlled systems.
- **Risk Register Integration:** Each permit links to identified hazards and control measures.
- **Safety Observations:** Front-line staff log near-misses through mobile forms, with patterns analysed weekly.
- **Toolbox Synchronization:** Every shift begins with a documented pre-task risk talk linked to the day's PTW.

Performance Metric

Permit Compliance % = (Valid Permits / Required Permits) X 100

Target 98% or higher. Anything less demands immediate root-cause review. Digital dashboards flag overdue permits and identify the responsible line of authority.

Safety is not the cost of doing work, it is the condition that allows work to continue.

Compliance: Making Standards Visible

Compliance ensures that what is promised in procedures is proven in practice.

Implementation Layers

- **Policy Compliance:** Adherence to ISO 9001 (QMS) and ISO 45001 (OHSMS) frameworks.
- **Process Compliance:** Auditable evidence for each stage gate, including material, work, QA, and billing.
- **Behaviour Compliance:** Leadership walk-downs and Stop-Work Authority embedded in culture.

- **Digital Compliance:** Dashboards integrating QA status, permit readiness, and risk closure.

Key Dashboards

- **HSE Readiness Index** = (Open Permits + Approved PPE + Toolbox % Compliance) / 3

- **Quality Closure Rate** = (Closed NCRs / Total NCRs) × 100

- **Audit Action Closure Time** ≤ 10 days average

Compliance converts invisible discipline into visible metrics, making leadership oversight factual rather than verbal.

Digital Integration

Modern Execution Control Links Quality and HSE modules with ERP and field applications while maintaining alignment with client-controlled systems such as the Permit-to-Work (PTW) platform. Instead of direct integration, the focus is on digital synchronisation. This ensures that internal readiness, QA checks, and performance metrics reflect the latest approved field activities.

Flow Example:

- Internal safety readiness completed and logged in ERP
- PTW issued by client, and the reference number entered into the internal PTW Log.
- Linked risk controls displayed on the internal dashboard for team awareness.
- Work executed, QA check completed, and SPI, CPI, and ECR automatically updated in ERP.
- Audit trail archived, with corrective actions and training feedback triggered.

This creates a real-time alignment loop between safety, quality, and performance indicators. It works not by merging systems but by ensuring that each platform mirrors the same truth.

The result is one ecosystem of accountability where client control and contractor discipline operate in perfect coordination.

Leadership Integration

Leaders reinforce control by:

- Reviewing Quality and Safety KPIs alongside cost and schedule each week.
- Making HSE leaders' part of production meetings rather than guests.
- Rewarding proactive reporting instead of silence.
- Treating every compliance failure as a system learning, not an individual fault.

When quality and safety are discussed in the same sentence as productivity, control becomes culture.

> **Leadership Reflection:** *Quality is proof of discipline, Safety is proof of foresight, and Compliance is proof of integrity. Control is not achieved when incidents stop happening, it is achieved when learning never stops happening. A project is truly under control when excellence, safety, and integrity share the same dashboard.*

11. Control Cycle: From Plan to Performance

Control is rhythm: Every day, data must turn into dialogue, and dialogue must turn into decisions. This is how leadership transforms planning from a document into a discipline. The control cycle is not a report, it is a conversation that happens every 24 hours.

Control Cycle Framework

Collect Daily Progress: Control starts with visibility. Field engineers capture actual quantities, man-hours, and inspection results before shift close. The data flows into digital dashboards, converting daily effort into measurable evidence. Every recorded entry builds the foundation for performance visibility.

Compare to Baseline (SPI / CPI): Leadership measures reality against plan through Earned Value Management (EVM).

- SPI (Schedule Performance Index) = EV / PV
- CPI (Cost Performance Index) = EV / AC

SPI < 1 means the project is behind schedule.

CPI < 1 means it is over cost.

Early variance detection prevents cumulative drift.

Find Variance Cause: Variances are not just numbers, they are signals. Identify root causes such as manpower shortfall, rework, material delay, or unplanned scope, and classify each as recoverable, non-recoverable, or systemic for a targeted response.

Recover within 48 Hours: Leadership intervention within two working days is essential to stop variance from turning into deviation. The recovery actions include:

- **Shift balancing:** add or stagger shifts to regain lost hours.
- **Re-sequencing:** advance non-dependent work while bottlenecks clear.
- **Resource reallocation:** redirect crews or equipment to the critical path.
- **Fast-track approval:** clear pending design or scope decisions immediately.

Update Forecast: Revise short-term (weekly) and mid-term (monthly) forecasts using current data. Keep SPI and CPI trends realistic and feed them into predictive dashboards so leaders can anticipate outcomes rather than react to them.

Cycle Integration

This control loop connects Field, Planning, Finance, and Leadership every day. When done well, it converts projects from reactive status-chasing to proactive stability.

Example: A 0.85 SPI detected on Day 6 led to manpower reallocation by Day 8, restoring SPI to 0.98 by Day 12, before management escalation was required.

> *Leadership Reflection: Control is a daily conversation, not a monthly report. The best leaders do not ask, What happened? They ask, What is happening now, and how are we correcting it? Control is not about finding delay, it is about preventing surprise.*

12. Earned Value and Cost Performance

Cost performance is where planning meets reality. Earned Value Management (EVM) converts work and spending into measurable truth.

Term	Full Form	Meaning / Purpose
EV	Earned Value	Budgeted cost of work actually completed. Measures progress achieved.
AC	Actual Cost	Money actually spent to date. Tracks real expenditure.
CPI	Cost Performance Index = EV / AC	Indicates cost efficiency: 1 = on budget, < 1 = overrun, and > 1 = savings.

Example: If the Budget at Completion (BAC) is 1,000,000 USD and the CPI is 0.95, then the Estimate at Completion (EAC) is:

EAC (Estimate at Completion) = BAC / CPI = 1,052,631 USD.

That 5% deviation is an early warning signal that leadership must act upon.

> *"Numbers do not lie, they simply wait to be interpreted."*

13. Interface & Coordination

Interfaces are invisible handovers where departments meet and delays often hide. Weekly coordination reviews expose friction before it spreads across the schedule.

Interface	Owner	Dependent	Typical Impact
Fabrication and QC	Workshop	QA / QC	Inspection delay
QC and Client	QA / QC	Client	Approval hold
E&I and Mechanical	E&I	Mechanical	Testing lag

Coordination meetings are not ceremonies, they are control checkpoints.

14. Forecasting & Recovery Planning

Forecasting turns measurement into action. If the Schedule Performance Index (SPI) is 0.92 at 60% progress, the project is 8% behind schedule.

Key Metric

Forecast Completion Index (FCI) = BAC / EAC

- FCI < 1 means risk of overrun
- FCI = 1 means the project is on budget
- FCI > 1 means an efficient trend

Rule: If SPI × CPI < 0.9, it means a recovery plan should be triggered.

Forecasting without recovery is diagnosis without treatment.

15. Digital Execution Control Cockpit

All control data converges into a single digital cockpit, one dashboard and one truth.

System	Purpose
ERP	Cost, procurement, and inventory tracking
Power BI	SPI / CPI dashboards & trend analysis
Barcode App	Real-time man-hour & job tracking
AI Model	Delay prediction & productivity analytics
Permit Tool	Safety compliance & authorization control
QA Cloud	Inspection traceability & document control

Digital visibility transforms leadership from reactive review to predictive response.

16. Baseline vs Actual Performance

Baseline comparison keeps progress honest.

Metric	Baseline	Actual	Variance
Duration	30 days	33 days	+3 days
SPI	1.00	0.92	Lagging
CPI	1.00	0.97	Cost pressure

Re-baselining is permitted only when approved by leadership, never as a routine. It records deliberate decisions, not excuses.

17. Feedback Loop to Estimation

Control without feedback is noise. Variance data such as man-hours, waste factors, and vendor reliability flow back to estimation. Within six months, structured feedback improved estimation accuracy by 8%.

> *Lesson: Control today creates credibility tomorrow. Every closed variance makes the next estimate wise.*

18. Planning Culture: Reactive to Predictive

Culture	Behaviour	Outcome
Reactive	Acts after issues occur	Stress & Overtime
Predictive	Plans for uncertainty	Calm & Confidence

Predictive culture rewards preparation, not heroics. Leaders who normalize anticipation eliminate the need for emergency brilliance.

Preparation is invisible excellence.

19. Routine vs Shutdown Scenarios

Scenario	Duration	Schedule SPI %	Productivity (CPI)	Utilization %
Routine Job	30 Days	97 %	1.08	95 %
Shutdown Job	10 Days	92 %	1.20	99 %

Routine work favours consistency, while shutdowns demand intensity. Predictive planning balances both, ensuring that urgency never replaces control.

Pressure reveals maturity. Planning preserves it.

20. Execution KPIs Summary

KPI	Formula	Target	Purpose
SPI	EV ÷ PV	≥ 1.0	Schedule Efficiency
CPI	EV ÷ AC	≥ 1.0	Cost Control
MHR (Man-hour Reliability)	On-time ÷ Total	≥ 95 %	Workforce Reliability

KPI	Formula	Target	Purpose
RUR (Resource Utilization Rate)	(Actual / Planned) × 100	90–105 %	Manpower Balance
EAR (Equipment Availability Rate)	Operating / Total hours	≥ 95 %	Equipment Readiness
Permit Compliance	Valid / Required	≥ 98 %	Safety Discipline
TRIR (Total Recordable Incident Rate)	(Incidents × 1 M) / Man-hours	< 0.5	Zero Harm
Cost Variance (CV)	EV – AC	≥ 0	Profitability

These KPIs form the factual, transparent, repeatable scorecard of Execution Control.

21. Control vs monitoring

Control	Monitoring
Proactive, acts before deviation	Reactive, records after deviation
Focuses on root causes	Focuses on status
Empowers decisions	Observes people
Continuous loop	Periodic review
Creates ownership	Checks compliance

Essence: Monitoring tells you what happened. Control ensures it will not.

Leadership that controls proactively rarely needs to monitor reactively.

22. Quick Formula Reference: Execution Metrics

Metric	Formula	Interpretation
EV	% Complete × Budget	Value earned to date
PV	Planned % × Budget	Planned value till date
AC	Actual Spending	Money spent
SPI	EV / PV	Schedule Efficiency
CPI	EV / AC	Cost Efficiency
BAC	Total Planned Cost	Budget at Completion
EAC	BAC / CPI	Forecast Total Cost
FCI	BAC / EAC	Overall Performance Trend

These quick references keep field teams numerically fluent, turning data into dialogue across all levels.

23. Leadership Reflection

Execution Control is where strategy meets discipline. Leaders who see problems before they appear never need to supervise, they simply guide the rhythm of control.

> **Final Thought:** Precision in vision becomes power in execution when leadership turns anticipation into action.

Chapter 6: Job Completion and Billing Preparation

AG Business Flow Framework™

"A job isn't complete until its evidence is complete."

1. Introduction: Lessons from "The Lost Dossier"

Back in Chapter 1, The Lost Dossier revealed how one missing, signed document delayed an entire project's close-out and revenue recognition. That story was never about paperwork, it was about integrity.

This chapter revisits that lesson with operational depth. Job completion is not the end of execution, it is the beginning of commercial validation. A valve may be overhauled, a weld may pass inspection, but until the evidence of completion is verified, signed, and stored, the organisation cannot translate effort into value.

The Job Completion and Billing Preparation phase is the bridge between operations and finance, where physical work becomes financial confirmation. It ensures every project leaves behind an unbroken trail of technical proof, quality endorsement, and commercial legitimacy.

> *Leadership Reflection: Completion is not paperwork, it is organisational integrity documented.*

2. The Transition from Execution to Completion

Completion begins when the defined scope is fully delivered. Yet true confirmation happens only when every responsible department, including Operations, QA/QC, and Finance, verifies that delivery through documented evidence. This is the moment when execution ends and value realisation begins.

Completion Flow

- **Operational Completion**: Work is finished and verified internally by the execution team. All punch lists are cleared, and equipment and materials are properly accounted for.

- **Quality Clearance:** QA/QC validates workmanship against standards, closes non-conformities, and issues inspection records. Conformance builds confidence.

- **Client Acceptance:** The authorised client representative reviews and signs the completion certificates or service sheets. That signature converts performance into entitlement for billing.

- **Documentation Compilation:** All supporting evidence, including reports, test certificates, calibration sheets, timesheets, and photos, is compiled into a digital Completion Package. This becomes the proof of delivery and quality.

- **Finance Validation:** Quantities, unit rates, and purchase order clauses are verified for alignment. Finance ensures that what is claimed matches what was contracted and approved.

Only after these five checkpoints does a job qualify to pass the Completion Gate, the point where technical closure turns into financial eligibility.

> **Leadership Insight:** *Completion is the handshake between performance and proof. When evidence moves as fast as*

execution, cash flow becomes predictable and credibility becomes visible.

3. The Completion Gate

The Completion Gate is the organisation's internal checkpoint that protects against premature billing. It requires sequential validation from all key functions, including Operations, QA/QC, and Finance, before any project is released for invoicing.

This gate ensures that technical truth always comes before financial claim. It is not a delay mechanism, it is a credibility mechanism.

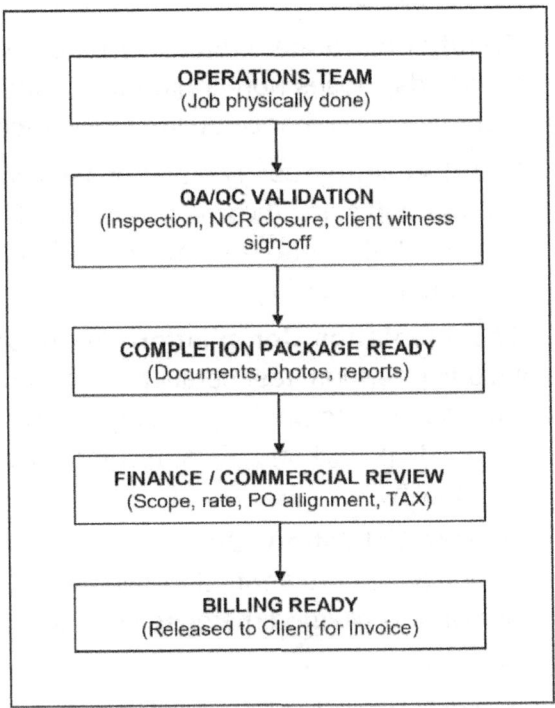

OPERATIONS TEAM
(Job physically done)

QA/QC VALIDATION
(Inspection, NCR closure, client witness sign-off

COMPLETION PACKAGE READY
(Documents, photos, reports)

FINANCE / COMMERCIAL REVIEW
(Scope, rate, PO allignment, TAX)

BILLING READY
(Released to Client for Invoice)

Figure 5 - Completion Gate

The alignment checkpoint between Operations, QA/QC, and Finance.

Each stage functions as a control barrier:

- **Operations** confirm that physical work is complete and internally verified.

- **QA/QC** validate inspection results, NCR closures, and client witness sign-off.

- **Completion Package** consolidates all supporting evidence, including drawings, photos, test reports, and calibration records.

- **Finance and Commercial** verify contractual compliance by reviewing scope, quantities, rates, PO alignment, and taxation.

Only when all validations are complete is the job declared Billing Ready and formally released for invoicing.

> *Leadership Reflection: The Completion Gate is not formality, it is discipline in sequence. When organisations make evidence the gatekeeper of revenue, integrity becomes their strongest financial control.*

4. Completion Verification and Inter-Department Validation

Verification ensures that what was built truly matches what was promised and that it complies with every approved specification. It serves as the bridge between execution and billing, where Operations confirm scope, QA/QC confirm quality, and Finance confirm commercial accuracy. No project should proceed to billing without this three-way validation.

Verification Matrix

Function	Verification Focus	Output
Operations	Scope completion, resource utilization, and punch-list clearance	Completion Memo

Function	Verification Focus	Output
QA / QC	Compliance to standards, inspection record verification, NCR closure	Inspection Report and Release Note
Finance / Commercial	Billing eligibility, PO and rate alignment, tax verification	Billing Approval Note

A weekly Completion Review Meeting brings these three functions together before any billing authorisation is issued. This structured review:

- Prevents disputes over quantities or approvals.
- Ensures documentation is complete before invoice release.
- Reinforces cross-functional accountability.

When Operations, QA/QC, and Finance validate one another's readiness, the result is zero ambiguity at billing and complete confidence during audit or client review.

> *Leadership Reflection: Verification is the handshake between technical truth and financial trust. Organisations that validate before they invoice never argue after the bill.*

5. Case Example: QA/QC vs Operations Conflict

During a piping modification project, Operations declared the job complete and ready for billing. However, QA/QC withheld final sign-off, citing minor coating defects visible on several joints. Operations argued that the issue was cosmetic and that commercial release should proceed to maintain cash flow. What followed became a textbook example of balanced control, where both quality and finance were respected.

Resolution Path

- **Joint Inspection:** Operations and QA/QC conducted a joint review to assess and quantify the pending touch-up area.

- **Conditional Release:** QA/QC issued a Conditional Release Note that allowed billing to proceed while recording remarks on the minor pending work.

- **Client Acknowledgment:** The client accepted the completion certificate with a clear reference to the pending coating touch-up.

- **Final Closure:** Once the touch-up was completed, QA/QC updated the final record, closed all remarks, and confirmed full compliance.

Outcome

- Quality integrity was preserved.

- Cash flow remained unaffected.

- Both departments aligned on evidence, not opinion.

This incident reinforced a core truth of process-driven organisations: control is not about stopping work, it is about sequencing assurance.

> **Leadership Reflection:** *A mature system does not choose between speed and standards, it balances both. When departments act through evidence instead of ego, quality and finance stop competing and start cooperating.*

6. Documentation Integrity Principle (DIP)

In high-reliability organisations, execution is proven not by memory but by evidence. The Documentation Integrity Principle (DIP) defines how that evidence is captured, protected, and retrieved. It is more than a record-keeping rule, it is a cultural standard that reflects maturity in Execution Control.

Documentation Integrity Principle (DIP): If it is not documented, it is not done. If it is not retrievable, it is not reliable.

This principle ensures that every deliverable leaves behind a verifiable digital footprint that meets three essential criteria:

- **Completeness:** All required evidence, including drawings, inspection records, calibration sheets, and completion certificates, is captured and cross-referenced. No activity is marked as complete without its corresponding proof.

- **Authenticity:** Every record carries valid signatures, stamps, and version control. Digital audit trails must clearly show who approved what and when. Authenticity turns documentation from information into evidence.

- **Accessibility:** All records are stored in an indexed digital repository where they can be retrieved instantly for management review, client verification, or audit. A record that cannot be found when needed is as good as one that was never created.

Organisations that enforce DIP reduce revenue leakage, audit observations, and client disputes. More importantly, they replace dependence on memory with dependence on systems, which is the true sign of process-driven maturity.

> **Leadership Reflection:** *Integrity is not proven by promise, it is proven by record. When documentation becomes discipline, credibility becomes culture.*

7. Documentation Control & Record Storage

If the Documentation Integrity Principle (DIP) defines what must be preserved, Documentation Control defines how it must be preserved. Strong documentation control ensures that every record, whether technical, commercial, or quality-related, remains traceable, auditable, and protected for future reference.

Key Practices

- **Unique Job and Document Numbering:** Each project and record must carry a unique identifier (for example, JCC-AG-2025-074) to maintain traceability across departments and archives.

- **Standardized Templates:** All reports, certificates, and logs must comply with ISO 9001. This ensures consistency, uniform presentation, and reliability of evidence.

- **Internal Completeness Checklists:** Before forwarding any completion dossier to Finance, an internal checklist confirms that all supporting records, including drawings, inspection reports, time logs, and client approvals, are complete and properly signed.

- **Centralized Storage Systems:** Use digital repositories such as SharePoint, Google Drive, or ERP-DMS platforms to maintain a single, authoritative source of documentation. Centralisation prevents data loss, duplication, and version confusion.

- **Automated Workflows:** Implement automated folder creation and version tracking to manage the entire document lifecycle, from draft to review, approval, and archival. Each workflow should record timestamps and user actions to ensure full audit traceability.

- **Access Control & Data Retention:** Restrict file permissions based on role and project involvement. Schedule periodic backups, both cloud and local, to safeguard institutional memory and maintain business continuity.

Audit Readiness

Organisations that enforce DIP reduce revenue leakage, audit observations, and client disputes. More importantly, they replace dependence on memory with dependence on systems, which is the true sign of process-driven maturity.

> *Leadership Reflection:* Integrity is not proven by promise, it is proven by record. When documentation becomes discipline, credibility becomes culture.

8. Dashboard Visibility and Performance Metrics

A Completion Dashboard transforms project status into visible accountability. It enables leaders to measure how effectively Operations, QA/QC, and Finance convert completed work into billable value. Every number on this dashboard represents speed, alignment, and reliability.

Completion Dashboard: Key Metrics

Metric	Target	Definition / Insight
Jobs Pending QA/QC Clearance	≤ 3	The number of completed jobs awaiting QA/QC sign-off. Measures technical closure speed. A rising count indicates inspection backlog or slow NCR resolution.
Jobs Awaiting Client Sign-off	≤ 5	The number of jobs technically cleared but still pending client acceptance. Reflects commercial alignment and client responsiveness. Persistent delays here signal weak communication or documentation gaps.
Average Days from Completion to Billing	≤ 7 days	The average time between internal completion approval and invoice submission. Indicates cash-flow efficiency. A higher value means documentation or finance validation is delaying revenue realization.

How to Use the Dashboard

- **Daily U pdate and W eekly Review:** The dashboard updates automatically each day and is reviewed weekly by project and finance leaders.
- **Colour Coding:**
  - **Green -** Within target
  - **Yellow -** At risk (50–80% of limit)

- o **Red** - Exceeds target and requires immediate escalation

- **Ownership:**
  - o **QA/QC Head** - Owns clearance backlog.
  - o **Project Manager** - Owns client sign-off status.
  - o **Finance** - Owns completion-to-billing duration.

Leadership Review: Trends are discussed in the weekly Completion Review Meeting, where attention shifts from blame to process correction.

Strategic Impact

When used consistently, the dashboard becomes a performance mirror that reveals not just where the project stands but how predictable the organisation has become. It links technical discipline with financial velocity, ensuring that efficiency remains both visible and measurable.

Leadership Reflection: Metrics are not for control, they are for clarity. What gets seen gets solved, and what gets measured gets managed.

9. Completion Gate Checklist

Before any job moves from execution to invoicing, it must pass a series of verifications that confirm technical truth, documentation integrity, and commercial accuracy. This is the Completion Gate Checklist, the practical control tool that prevents premature billing and ensures every invoice is backed by verified evidence.

Completion Gate Checklist

Verification Item	Status
Operations confirmed full physical completion	☐
QA/QC clearance issued and all NCRs closed	☐

Verification Item	Status
Client completion certificate reviewed and signed	☐
Timesheets and measurement sheets verified for accuracy	☐
Material reconciliation completed and approved	☐
Variation orders, if any, attached and cross-referenced	☐
All documents digitally stored and properly indexed	☐
Commercial validation of rates, quantities, and scope	☐
Finance verification of tax, PO, and cost codes	☐
Completion package officially tagged as Billing Ready	☐

Each item represents a control barrier that must be passed before the job enters the billing cycle. Once all boxes are checked, the project achieves completion integrity, meaning every claimed value is supported by both technical and financial proof.

> **Leadership Reflection:** *The Completion Gate Checklist is not paperwork, it is the final quality test of credibility. When billing begins with verification, payment begins with trust.*

10. Management Perspective: Completion as a Financial Checkpoint

From a management perspective, completion lag equals cash-flow lag. Every day that a technically completed job remains unverified or undocumented is another day of delayed revenue recognition.

By institutionalising the Completion Gate and the Documentation Integrity Principle (DIP), leaders convert project control into predictable revenue flow. Completion becomes more than an operational milestone, it becomes a financial checkpoint.

Key Success Enablers

- **KPI - Average Days to Billing Readiness:** Track the time gap between physical completion and invoice release. Target seven days or less for healthy cash velocity.

- **Weekly Review Meetings (Operations + Finance):** Align teams on pending completions, sign-off bottlenecks, and documentation gaps. Consistent visibility keeps progress moving.

- **Reward Systems for Zero Pending Documentation:** Recognise departments or individuals who maintain on-time completion packages. Encourage accountability through appreciation rather than enforcement.

- **Audit Logs for Gate Approvals:** Maintain digital records showing who approved what and when. This traceability strengthens audit confidence and prevents post-billing disputes.

When completion control becomes part of daily leadership routine, cash-flow predictability stops being a financial target and starts becoming an organisational habit.

> **Leadership Reflection:** *Control builds credibility, and credibility builds cash flow. The fastest way to accelerate revenue is to finish proof, not just work.*

11. Transition to Invoicing

The output of this phase, the Completion Package, becomes the official input for the next phase, the Invoicing Process. Every verified document, signature, and inspection report flows directly into invoice generation, ensuring that what is billed is indisputable proof of the work performed.

The Completion Package includes:

- Client-signed Completion Certificates

- QA/QC Release Notes and Inspection Reports
- Verified Timesheets and Measurement Sheets
- Approved Material Reconciliation Logs
- Commercial Validation Notes and Rate Confirmations

Together, these records form the backbone of billing, converting operational achievement into recognised revenue. Once this dossier is approved by Finance and tagged as Billing Ready, it moves seamlessly into the invoicing workflow without the need for re-verification or delay.

> *Leadership Reflection: Billing accuracy is built upstream, not at the finance desk. When every invoice begins with proof, revenue moves with the same pace as reliability.*

12. Leadership Reflection

Leaders who uphold the Documentation Integrity Principle (DIP) understand that technical closure means nothing without documentation closure. Every stamped certificate, approved log, and archived record is not just evidence, it is currency.

Through the Completion Gate, an organisation transforms activity into accountability and accountability into revenue. When leaders make documentation part of culture rather than compliance, they turn reliability into financial strength.

The proof of work is not in what was done, it is in what can be shown, signed, and sustained.

Chapter 7: Invoicing Process

AG Business Flow Framework™

"A perfect invoice is a reflection of process discipline."

1. The Invoice That Waited

A shutdown crew at an oil refinery completed its work a week ahead of schedule. The client signed the Service Entry Sheet (SES) and commended the team for their efficiency. Yet, somewhere between the site and the head office, the signed SES sat quietly in a supervisor's email draft, unsent.

Forty-five days later, the project manager realised that the invoice had never been submitted. The work was finished. The client was satisfied. But the payment was still pending.

It was not negligence. It was a process gap. The company possessed technical brilliance but lacked financial discipline. That single incident became a turning point, giving rise to a new internal principle: Financial Integrity, a culture where every invoice reflects accuracy, compliance, and accountability.

In a process-driven organisation, financial closure carries the same importance as operational completion.

> **Leadership Reflection:** *A job is only complete when its value is realised. Process integrity is not just about finishing work, it is about completing revenue.*

2. The Essence of Financial Integrity

Financial integrity begins when data, documentation, and discipline align. An invoice is not a financial formality, it is the mirror of organisational reliability. It reflects how seamlessly Operations, Estimation, and Finance work together in rhythm.

When an organisation treats invoicing as a compliance-driven process rather than a cash-driven race, it gains more than speed, it earns trust.

Purpose of Financial Integrity

- **To ensure accurate revenue recognition:** Every invoice must represent work that is contractually valid, technically verified, and commercially approved.

- **To establish traceability from scope to payment:** Each billed item should link directly to the originating scope, estimate, and purchase order without ambiguity.

- **To maintain transparency between departments:** Shared data and open workflows eliminate confusion and build accountability across the value chain.

- **To guarantee tax and statutory compliance:** Proper documentation and timely submission protect the organisation from penalties and credibility loss.

3. The Invoicing Workflow

A structured workflow forms the backbone of invoicing discipline. It ensures that every invoice issued is traceable, validated, and compliant. It is the natural continuation of the Completion Gate process.

Invoicing Flow

- **Job Completion Confirmation:** The process begins with a signed Job Completion Certificate (JCC) or Service Entry Sheet (SES) received from Operations. This is the official trigger for billing readiness.

- **Billing Compilation:** The Billing or Commercial team consolidates all supporting documents, including QA/QC release notes, timesheets, material reconciliations, and client acknowledgements.

- **Invoice Drafting:** Using verified data, the Commercial or Finance team prepares a draft invoice within the ERP system, linking it to the correct project code and purchase order reference.

- **Review & Approvals:** he draft undergoes cross-functional validation.

  - **Commercial or Project Controls:** Confirms rates, scope, and purchase order alignment against approved estimates.

  - **QA/QC:** Confirms quality clearance and client acceptance.

  - **Finance:** Verifies cost codes, taxes, and compliance.

- **Authorization & Issue:** The approved invoice is digitally signed, stamped, and released by authorised signatories in accordance with the delegation matrix or financial policy.

- **Submission & Acknowledgment:** The invoice is submitted to the client by portal, email, or hard copy and tracked until formal acknowledgement or receipt confirmation is obtained.

Each step creates an auditable trail, a visible chain of reliability that connects execution, evidence, and earnings. A disciplined workflow prevents disputes, accelerates approval, and demonstrates the financial integrity of a mature organisation.

Leadership Reflection: An invoice is not paperwork, it is the final proof of process. When workflow becomes habit, accuracy becomes automatic.

4. The 3-Level Accuracy Verification

Financial integrity depends on one essential foundation, accuracy at every level. The Three-Level Verification Framework ensures that each invoice is validated contractually, operationally, and fiscally before it reaches the client.

Three-Level Verification Framework

Level	Verification Focus	Responsible Function	Purpose
Level 1 PO Accuracy	Validate rates, quantities, and scope against the Purchase Order or Contract.	Commercial / Project Controls	Ensures commercial correctness and contractual traceability.
Level 2 SES / JCC Accuracy	Confirm executed work, client approvals, and signed acceptance certificates.	Operations / QA & QC	Ensures physical and technical correctness.
Level 3 Tax & Ledger Accuracy	Verify VAT %, QR code, ledger posting, and accounting entry compliance.	Finance	Ensures fiscal and statutory correctness.

All three levels must align before an invoice is numbered or issued. If any checkpoint is incomplete, the invoice must pause, because speed without validation is risk disguised as efficiency.

> *Leadership Reflection: Three approvals do not delay an invoice, they protect a company's integrity. Accuracy is not formality, it is the discipline that turns confidence into cash flow.*

5. Pre-Invoicing Validation Framework

Each invoice must pass through a defined series of pre-checks that confirm accuracy, compliance, and accountability before submission.

Validation Point	Purpose
Scope and quantity verification	Confirms billable work matches approved contract
Rate verification	Ensures pricing integrity
Supporting document completeness	Proof of performance
Tax verification	Compliance with regulatory requirements
Sequential numbering	Control and traceability
Approval sign-offs	Accountability and authorization

Validation transforms operational output into financial legitimacy.

6. Departmental Coordination Matrix

Invoicing is a coordinated process that depends on every department working in sequence. Each function plays a specific role in ensuring that the invoice represents both technical truth and financial accuracy.

Department	Key Role	Deliverable
Operations	Provide evidence of completion	JCC / SES
Commercial / Project Control	Verify rates and contract terms	PO Cross-check
Finance	Apply VAT, generate invoice, and ledger posting	Tax-compliant invoice

Department	Key Role	Deliverable
QA/QC	Verify that quality completion matches client expectations	Signed QA release
Document Control	Maintain archives and dispatch logs	Invoice file and acknowledgment

Invoicing is a relay race, not a solo sprint. Every department must pass the baton on time.

7. The Structure of a Perfect Invoice

A compliant invoice must contain all the information needed to verify accuracy, traceability, and authenticity.

Required Details

- Company and client information, including VAT numbers
- Invoice number and date
- Purchase Order or Contract reference
- Description of service or supply provided
- Quantity, unit rate, subtotal
- VAT % and total value
- Bank details (IBAN, SWIFT, Account Name)
- Authorized signature and company stamp
- Attachments such as JCC, Delivery Notes, timesheets, variation approvals

Rule of thumb: An invoice should answer every client question before it is asked.

8. Electronic Invoicing and Tax Compliance

Digital invoicing is now a regulatory requirement in most countries. Modern e-invoicing systems ensure transparency, traceability, and compliance across every transaction. Each invoice must:

- Contain a QR code and digital signature.

- Be generated from an approved e-invoicing platform.
- Synchronise with tax authority servers in real time.
- Be stored electronically for a 10 of ten years or depending on local legal and tax regulations.

Compliance failures can cause reputational damage far greater than financial penalties. Financial integrity requires readiness, not reaction.

> **Leadership Reflection:** *Tax accuracy is not an accounting skill, it is a leadership responsibility.*

9. Common Invoicing Scenarios

Different projects require different billing structures, but the principle remains the same: evidence before earnings. Regardless of contract type, every invoice must be supported by documentation that proves work completion, compliance, and approval.

Invoicing Formats and Their Control Focus

Scenario	Description	Control Focus / Attachments
Lump Sum Jobs	A single invoice raised upon total job completion.	Requires the full Completion Package, including JCC or SES, QA/QC release, and client sign-off.
Unit Rate Jobs	Periodic billing based on measured quantities or output units.	Attach measurement sheets, approved quantity logs, and rate confirmations.
Time and Material (T&M)	Billing based on actual labour hours and material usage.	Supported by timesheets, material slips, and client countersignatures.

Scenario	Description	Control Focus / Attachments
Progress Billing	Milestone-based invoicing linked to project stages or completion percentages.	Attach milestone certificates, progress reports, and client verifications.
Retention Billing	Invoicing for retained value released after the warranty or performance period.	Requires a release certificate or client clearance note.

Each format changes the attachments but never the principle. The process must prove that work was completed, verified, and approved before value is claimed.

> *Leadership Reflection: Invoicing may vary by contract, but integrity has only one form. The discipline of documentation is what turns every billing model into a trusted transaction.*

10. Common Invoicing Delays and How to Prevent Them

Even the most accurate invoice can stall if supporting controls are weak. Most delays arise not from system failures but from process gaps and communication breakdowns between departments. The key to financial integrity is anticipating these issues before they occur.

Typical Delay Scenarios and Preventive Measures

Root Cause	Impact	Preventive Measure
Missing JCC / SES	Client rejection or delayed approval	Link job closure in ERP to mandatory upload of signed JCC / SES before billing.

Root Cause	Impact	Preventive Measure
PO Mismatch	Invoice resubmission and payment deferral	Verify PO number, revision, and line-item match before invoice draft.
Incomplete Attachments	Delay in internal and client approval	Use a standard invoice checklist to confirm all supporting documents.
Tax / Entity Errors	Compliance breach or regulatory penalty	Ensure Finance verification of tax details and entity codes before release.
Internal Approval Lag	Missed client payment window	Adopt digital approval workflows with automated alerts and escalation triggers.

Proactive control of these five areas not only prevents billing delays but also strengthens client confidence and cash-flow predictability.

> *Leadership Reflection: Delays rarely come from systems, they come from silence between departments. Communication closes gaps faster than reminders ever will.*

11. Supporting Documents: Proof Before Payment

Every invoice must be supported by verifiable evidence that connects scope, completion, and cost. These documents convert billing from a claim into confirmation, turning assumptions into auditable proof.

Required Supporting Documents

- **Signed JCC / SES:** Confirms job completion and client acceptance.

- **Purchase Order or Service Order:** Defines contractual scope, rates, and terms.

- **Delivery Notes / Material Slips:** Validate materials delivered or consumed at site.

- **Inspection / QA Release Reports:** Certify that quality and safety requirements were met.

- **Variation Order Approvals (if any):** Authorize changes in scope, price, or schedule.

- **Timesheets (for T&M Jobs):** Provide evidence of actual labour hours worked.

- **Tax Certificate or Registration Copy:** Ensures compliance with statutory and VAT regulations.

Document control turns billing from assumption into authentication. Each attachment strengthens the credibility of the invoice, ensuring that payment approval is based on proof, not persuasion.

> **Leadership Reflection:** *A complete invoice does not need follow-up, it speaks for itself. When documentation becomes evidence, payment becomes predictable.*

12. The Invoice Quality Gate

Before dispatch, every invoice must pass through the Invoice Quality Gate, a structured verification stage that aligns operational, commercial, and fiscal accuracy. This checkpoint ensures that no invoice leaves the organisation without proof, validation, and authorisation.

Invoice Quality Gate Checklist

Checkpoint	Responsibility	Status
Job completion evidence attached	Operations	☐
PO reference and scope verified	Commercial / Project Controls	☐
VAT rate and QR code validated	Finance	☐
Sequential invoice number logged	Administration	☐

Checkpoint	Responsibility	Status
Attachments merged and archived	Document Control	☐
Authorized signature applied	Management / Approving Authority	☐

Only when all items are checked does the invoice proceed to client submission. This final control step eliminates rejections, prevents duplication, and strengthens accountability. It is the hallmark of financial predictability, the highest form of process maturity.

> *Leadership Reflection:* A Quality Gate turns good documentation into great discipline. The more predictable the process, the more powerful the trust it creates.

13. Internal Controls and Authorization

Every invoice must pass through defined authorisation levels before release. This structure ensures segregation of duties, prevents unauthorised billing, and protects both the organisation and its leadership from compliance risks.

Approval Matrix

Invoice Value (USD)	Approval Authority
≤ USD 50,000	Project Manager
USD 50,001 – 250,000	Functional Head
> USD 250,000	Director / Executive Management

Each level of control leaves behind a digital signature and timestamp, not to slow the process but to anchor accountability. Approvals move through digital workflows for transparency, traceability, and audit readiness.

This layered control structure ensures that no invoice depends on memory or manual oversight. Authorisation becomes institutional rather than individual.

> **Leadership Reflection:** *Controls do not restrict trust, they record it. Every digital approval is a visible act of responsibility, a sign that integrity has been built into the system.*

14. Invoice Dispatch and Acknowledgment

Once an invoice passes the Quality Gate and internal approvals, it must be formally dispatched and acknowledged by the client. The mode of submission depends on client requirements and contractual terms, but the principle remains the same: no dispatch without traceability.

Submission Methods

- **E-mail with Delivery Confirmation:** The simplest and fastest mode. Ensure that the delivery receipt or automatic acknowledgment is archived.
- **E-Portal Submission (via client-specific or third-party platforms)**: Upload all required attachments according to the portal checklist. Record the official submission ID and timestamp for traceability.
- **Hard Copy Submission:** Hand-deliver the invoice to the client's accounts or contract department and obtain a stamped acknowledgment copy as the official receipt.

The date of acknowledgment, whether digital or stamped, defines the start of the payment term. It must therefore be recorded in the Billing Tracker, capturing:

- Job Number / Project Code
- Invoice Number
- Dispatch Date

- Acknowledgment Date
- Acknowledgment Reference / Portal ID

This simple tracking habit transforms billing from reactive follow-up to predictive cash-flow management.

> **Leadership Reflection:** *Invoices do not move because they are raised, they move because they are received and recorded. Every acknowledgment date is a commitment timestamp. Track it, and your cash flow will never surprise you.*

15. Case Example: The Corrective Invoicing Campaign

Background

A leading fabrication firm discovered that nearly 40% of its invoices were delayed or returned by clients due to documentation gaps, mismatched data, or missing approvals. The problem was not lack of effort but lack of control. Invoices were being created faster than they were being verified.

Action Plan

To rebuild accuracy and restore client confidence, management launched a Corrective Invoicing Campaign built on four key initiatives:

- **Centralized Billing Tracker:** Introduced a shared dashboard between Operations, QA/QC, Commercial, and Finance for real-time visibility of invoice status.
- **Digital Signatures:** Removed physical bottlenecks and ensured every approval left a verifiable audit trail.
- **Weekly "Invoice Readiness" Meetings:** Cross-functional teams reviewed pending packages, cleared roadblocks, and tracked progress together.

- **Recognition Program:** Created a "First-Time-Right" award for teams that submitted invoices with zero corrections or rejections.

Outcome

- Invoice delay reduced from 40% to 8%.
- Client rejections dropped to below 1%.
- Average billing cycle time improved from 12 days to just 4 days.

The results proved a powerful truth: discipline, not software, builds efficiency. Technology amplified the change, but process clarity made it possible.

> **Leadership Reflection:** *Systems accelerate only what discipline sustains. The best financial reforms do not begin with tools, they begin with accountability.*

16. KPI Dashboard for Financial Integrity

Financial integrity becomes visible only when it can be measured. A well-defined KPI Dashboard tracks how efficiently the organisation converts execution into revenue, from job completion to cash realisation. These indicators serve as both a performance compass and a leadership control tool.

Key Performance Indicators

KPI	Purpose / Definition	Target
Invoice Cycle Time	Measures the duration from job completion to invoice submission. Reflects process responsiveness and coordination between Operations and Finance.	≤ 5 days
First-Time-Right %	Percentage of invoices accepted by the client without correction or rejection. Indicates documentation quality and internal review strength.	≥ 95 %

KPI	Purpose / Definition	Target
Billing Accuracy	Ratio of correct invoices to total invoices issued. Demonstrates validation effectiveness across the Quality Gate.	≥ 98 %
Rejection Rate	Percentage of invoices returned or disputed by the client. Lower values signify better clarity and compliance.	≤ 2 %
DSO (Days Sales Outstanding)	Measures cash realization speed, the average number of days between invoicing and payment receipt. Reflects overall financial discipline.	≤ Contract Term

These KPIs form the heartbeat of financial integrity. Tracking them weekly enables leaders to predict cash-flow behaviour, detect process drift early, and sustain financial reliability across projects.

> *Leadership Reflection: Numbers do not build integrity, consistency does. When KPIs are reviewed with discipline, financial control becomes a culture rather than a task.*

17. ERP Integration and Automation

As organisations mature, manual invoicing controls evolve into digitally orchestrated workflows. Enterprise systems such as Microsoft Dynamics, SAP, or workflow platforms like Make.com automate key invoicing steps, creating precision and traceability at scale.

Automation Capabilities

- **Auto-Populated Invoices:** Generate draft invoices automatically when a job reaches the "Billing Ready" status in the ERP system.
- **Automated Validation:** Built-in cross-checks ensure that PO numbers, VAT codes, and cost centres match contract and finance policies.

- **Triggered Approval Workflows:** Digital routing replaces manual follow-up. Each approval leaves a timestamp and a verifiable audit trail.

- **Digital Archiving:** Invoices, attachments, and acknowledgements are securely stored with version control for easy retrieval.

- **Real-Time KPI Dashboards:** System-generated analytics track cycle time, rejection rate, and DSO, enabling leaders to act on data rather than assumptions.

Automation enables precision at scale. It prevents slippage, standardises accuracy, and ensures that nothing is overlooked and everything is verified. Technology does not replace discipline, it replicates it consistently across every transaction.

> *Leadership Reflection:* Automation does not build integrity, it preserves it. When systems mirror process discipline, performance becomes predictable and trust becomes measurable.

18. Audit and Record Retention

Invoices are more than financial documents. They are legal records that reflect the organisation's integrity and compliance standards. Proper record retention protects against disputes, ensures transparency during audits, and preserves the company's credibility long after project completion.

Retention Requirement

- At least seven to ten years, depending on local legal and tax regulations.
- Applies to both digital and physical records, including invoices, approvals, supporting documents, and correspondence.

- Retention policies should comply with applicable tax, commercial, and data protection laws in the operating region.

Audit Essentials

- **Sequential Numbering (No Gaps):** Maintain continuous invoice numbering to ensure traceability and detect glitches.

- **Approved Supporting Documents:** Each invoice must include validated completion certificates, POs, QA/QC reports, and variation approvals.

- **Tax and Statutory Compliance:** Confirm correct tax percentages, registration details, and legally required disclosures for each jurisdiction.

- **Secure Digital Archiving:** Store all invoices in indexed repositories with controlled access, version history, and long-term backup for retrieval during audit or legal review.

A company that safeguards its financial records with the same discipline it applies to its engineering documentation demonstrates maturity that transcends industry boundaries. Good recordkeeping is not about formality, it is about continuity and credibility.

> *Leadership Reflection: Audits do not test memory, they test methods. When every invoice can be retrieved and verified years later, the organisation proves that reliability is not just practised, it is preserved.*

19. Communication Etiquette

An invoice is the company's voice in writing. It speaks long before finance or management ever follow up. How it is written, sent, and followed up reflects not only the organisation's process but also its professional character.

Best Practices for Invoice Communication

- **Attach a Cover Letter:** Include a short note summarising the project, purchase order reference, and total billing amount. Clarity invites faster action.

- **Use Neutral, Factual Language:** Keep the tone professional and objective. Avoid emotional or subjective wording, even during escalation.

- **Maintain a Correspondence Log:** Record every email, acknowledgement, and follow-up for traceability. Documented communication protects credibility.

- **Escalate Delays Politely but Persistently:** Courtesy sustains relationships while persistence ensures accountability. Always copy relevant stakeholders, not just individuals.

Communication reflects organisational character. A polite, precise follow-up today can secure tomorrow's opportunity, because professionalism is remembered long after payment is processed.

> **Leadership Reflection:** *Financial communication is not persuasion, it is professionalism on display. Every message about money should sound like the company it represents – clear, calm, and credible.*

20. Continuous Improvement

Financial integrity is a living system. It matures through reflection, feedback, and repetition. Sustaining accuracy and compliance requires more than procedures, it requires a culture that learns from its own data.

Monthly Invoice Review Meetings

Hold regular cross-functional reviews involving Operations, Finance, QA/QC, and Commercial teams to turn insights into improvements.

Agenda Focus:

- **Discuss Rejected Invoices:** Identify patterns, root causes, and corrective actions.

- **Update Templates and Tax Rules:** Ensure that forms and compliance standards reflect current regulations.

- **Share Best Practices:** Exchange success stories and lessons between departments and regions.

- **Recognize "Zero-Error" Performers:** Celebrate accuracy and ownership, and reward those who make reliability a habit.

Every review transforms routine into refinement. Continuous improvement in billing does not just accelerate cash flow, it strengthens organisational reliability.

> *Leadership Reflection: Every rejection carries a lesson, and every lesson builds resilience. The organisations that keep learning from their invoices never repeat the same mistake twice.*

21. Case Snapshot: Discipline Through Data

A maintenance contractor introduced a colour-coded invoicing dashboard to track billing readiness in real time.

- **Ready (green)** – All documents complete and approved.
- **Pending (yellow)** – Awaiting internal or client validation.
- **Delayed (red)** – Exceeded target submission date.

Within six months, delayed invoices dropped by 80 per cent, and the average billing cycle time fell below five days.

The system required no new policy, only visibility. Once everyone could see where the delay occurred, accountability became instinctive.

Leadership Reflection: Data does not control people, it reminds them. When information becomes visible, performance becomes voluntary.

22. Leadership Role in Financial Integrity

True financial integrity begins with leadership tone. No system, checklist, or KPI can replace the example set by leaders who view invoicing not as paperwork but as the organisation's statement of credibility.

Leaders Must:

- **Treat invoicing accuracy as a strategic KPI, not a clerical task:** Every delayed or rejected invoice reflects a gap in leadership oversight, not just team performance.

- **Review DSO and rejection rates monthly:** Consistent attention to these indicators turns financial health into a managed rhythm, not a quarterly surprise.

- **Encourage cross-departmental visibility:** When Finance, Operations, and Commercial teams see the same data, accountability becomes shared and proactive.

- **Reward speed with accuracy, not speed alone:** Recognize teams that deliver invoices right the first time. Accuracy builds trust, and speed builds stability only when it's disciplined.

Leadership does not merely sign invoices, it sets the rhythm for how responsibly they are created. When leaders make precision a habit and integrity a standard, invoicing ceases to be a transaction and becomes a reflection of organisational maturity.

Leadership Reflection: Leaders do not approve invoices, they approve culture. The tone they set in finance echoes through every department that follows their lead.

23. Precision Pointers for Zero-Error Billing

Operational excellence in billing is not achieved through complex systems but through repeatable precision. These seven discipline points turn process consistency into financial reliability.

Zero-Error Billing Checklist

- **Verify Early:** Align **PO, JCC/SES, and tax data** before invoice creation to prevent downstream corrections.

- **Standardize Templates:** Use uniform formats to reduce review time and minimize interpretation errors.

- **Track Daily:** Maintain an **invoice delay tracker** as an early-warning system for bottlenecks.

- **Digitize Workflows:** Enable approval speed with traceability through ERP or workflow tools.

- **Audit Regularly:** Convert every client rejection into internal training material.

- **Reward Accuracy:** Recognize teams that deliver "First-Time-Right" invoices to reinforce precision as culture.

- **Lead by Example:** Leadership participation in reviews drives accountability and shapes behaviour across teams.

Leadership Reflection: Precision is not perfection, it is discipline repeated until it becomes culture. When billing follows the same process every time, accuracy stops being an exception and starts being the norm.

24. Summary and Transition

Invoicing is where technical effort becomes financial truth. It reflects an organisation's capacity to convert work into worth, accurately, compliantly, and confidently.

When executed with precision:

- Revenue recognition becomes predictable.

- Cash flow becomes stable.
- Inter-departmental trust becomes natural.
- Clients begin to see professionalism as the default.

Financial integrity is not about perfection, it is about repeatable accuracy. Every invoice that passes through the Quality Gate carries proof that systems are working and that leadership values evidence over assumption.

As we move to Chapter 8: Payment Follow-Up and Collection, the focus shifts from recording earned value to realising it in cash, continuing the same discipline that began with the invoice itself.

> **Leadership Reflection:** *Financial integrity is complete only when cash confirms it in the bank. The discipline that built the invoice must now sustain the collection.*

Chapter 8: Payment Follow-Up and Collection

AG Business Flow Framework™

"Cash flow is not finance, it's operational closure."

1. Introduction

Cash flow is the final signature of operational discipline. A project may be executed flawlessly and invoiced perfectly, yet if payment is not collected on time, the process remains incomplete. In reality, payment follow-up is not an accounting activity, it is the act of closing operations with financial proof.

This phase of the AG Business Flow Framework™ forms the bridge between execution excellence and financial realisation. It tests not only the strength of systems but also the maturity of communication within the organisation and with clients.

When an organisation manages its receivables with structure, respect, and persistence, it builds more than liquidity, it builds credibility.

> **Leadership Reflection:** *Cash flow does not reward effort, it rewards consistency. Payment discipline is the visible result of invisible process control.*

2. The Foundation: Understanding Payment Triggers

Every project agreement contains a roadmap to its own cash flow. Recognising and tracking these payment triggers early ensures that collections are planned, not pursued. When triggers are documented, monitored, and assigned, cash flow becomes predictable and no longer relies on reminders or crisis follow-ups.

Common Payment Triggers

Trigger Type	Typical Release Condition
Advance Payment	Upon PO release, contract signing, or site readiness.
Progress Payment	At each milestone, progress percentage, or monthly billing cycle.
Retention	After Defects Liability Period (DLP) closure or client certification.
Final Settlement	Upon submission and acceptance of as-built dossiers, warranties, or final documentation.

These triggers must be digitally recorded within the ERP or billing tracker, linked to automated reminders and assigned owners. When every milestone is tracked systematically, payment follow-up becomes proactive instead of personal.

> *Leadership Reflection: Predictable cash flow begins with predictable triggers. The goal is simple: no payment should rely on memory.*

3. Internal Synergy: One Voice, One Process

Timely payment collection is a coordinated act, not an individual effort. Four departments, each with distinct roles, must work in unison to turn outstanding invoices into predictable inflows. When these functions communicate in harmony, clients hear structure, not confusion.

Roles in the Collection Process

Department	Role in Collection
Operations	Provide signed WCCs (Work Completion Certificates), timesheets, and inspection reports promptly after job closure.
Sales	Maintain client relationships, manage communication tone, and sense client sentiment for early issue detection.
Finance	Track receivables, issue reminders, and escalate delays as per the collection policy.
Management	Step in at strategic points to resolve escalated cases and reinforce accountability.

Discipline in communication flow matters as much as documentation. When the organisation speaks with one professional voice, clients perceive reliability. When departments act separately, clarity is lost and payment cycles extend.

> **Leadership Reflection:** Clients do not respond to pressure, they respond to professionalism. Unified communication turns reminders into results.

4. Communication Psychology: The Human Side of Collection

At its core, payment follow-up is about psychology, not pressure. Most payment delays arise from processes, not people. Clients usually postpone payments because of missing internal approvals, documentation mismatches, or budget cycles, not due to unwillingness to pay.

Understanding this changes the tone of follow-up from frustration to professionalism. Effective collection communication blends empathy with firmness, creating persistence without conflict.

Principles of Effective Communication Psychology

- **Respect before Request:** Begin with appreciation for the client's cooperation and partnership. Respect builds receptiveness.
- **Empathy before Escalation:** Recognise the client's internal challenges before requesting compliance. Understanding fosters cooperation.
- **Data before Emotion:** Quote invoice numbers, dates, and payment terms clearly. Facts speak louder than feelings.
- **Consistency before Confrontation:** Regular, composed reminders are far more effective than occasional forceful messages. Professional persistence always outperforms pressure.
- **Confidence without Threat:** Authority comes from process discipline, not personal tone. Calm assurance creates credibility.

When communication reflects respect, clarity, and consistency, clients view collection teams not as enforcers but as professionals maintaining order within a shared process.

> *Leadership Reflection: The best collectors do not chase money, they manage relationships. Respect turns reminders into results, and results sustain reputation.*

5. The Three-Level Escalation Ladder

A disciplined collection process depends on structured escalation, not spontaneous reaction. Each level has a distinct tone, purpose, and audience, moving from a courteous reminder to a policy-based action while maintaining professionalism and respect.

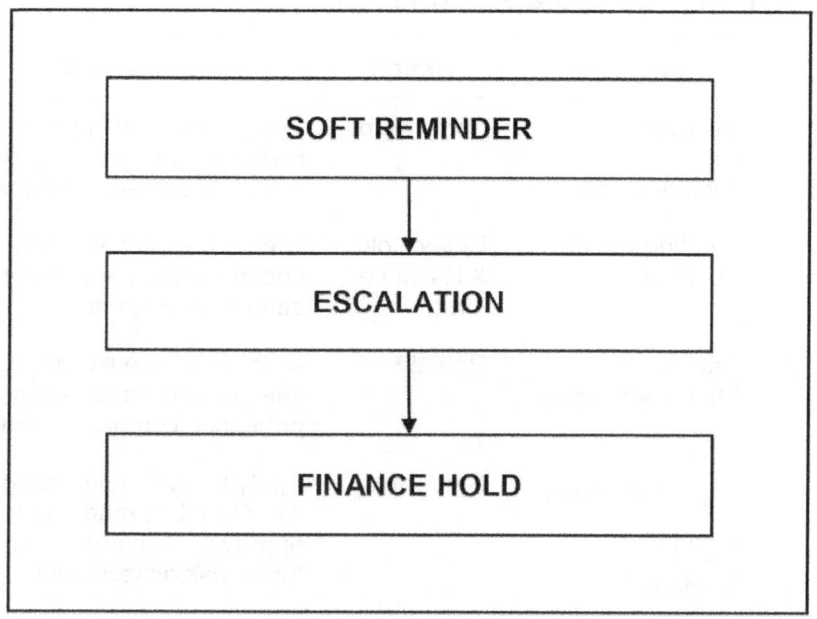

Figure 6 - Escalation Ladder

A Finance Hold must always be structured, reversible, and justified. It represents control, not conflict, and should be communicated with clarity, consistency, and calm authority.

> **Leadership Reflection:** *Escalation is not pressure, it is precision. When tone follows structure, even the firmest message earns respect instead of resistance.*

6. Finance Hold Decision Matrix

A Finance Hold should never be emotional. It must be data-driven, documented, and transparent. The following matrix defines when and how to apply financial holds without harming client relationships or disrupting operational continuity.

Finance Hold Decision Matrix

Scenario	Action	Remarks
Overdue > 45 days with full documentation	Apply Hold	Notify client and internal teams. Resume activities once payment acknowledgment is received.
Pending Client Approval	Delay Hold & Escalate First	Offer a meeting to resolve documentation or approval issues before enforcement.
Critical Site or Shutdown Support	Partial Hold	Maintain essential services only to safeguard client operations while protecting company liquidity.
Repeat Overdue Client (≥ 3 Incidents)	Strict Hold	Apply the hold immediately. New work requires management approval. Track client patterns for future risk assessment.

Transparency preserves relationships even during enforcement. When holds are applied with fairness, clear communication, and proper documentation, clients respect the discipline rather than resist it. A structured decision process prevents emotional escalation and strengthens long-term credibility.

> *Leadership Reflection: Escalation is not pressure, it is precision. When tone follows structure, even the firmest message earns respect instead of resistance.*

7. Case: The Client Who Remembered Respect

An EPC client had a pattern of delaying payments by more than sixty days. Instead of increasing the pressure, the company changed its tone. Every email began with appreciation and ended with an assurance of continued partnership.

A few weeks later, the client's finance manager shared a quiet truth: "We prioritised your payment first because your follow-ups were professional, never pressuring."

From that point onwards, payment regularity improved, and so did the relationship. What changed was not the policy or the procedure, it was the tone.

Lesson: In payment collection, tone is strategy. Clients may forget the amount or the deadline, but they never forget how they were treated.

> *Leadership Reflection: Respect accelerates response. The professionalism shown during payment follow-up determines whether clients see you as a partner or a pursuer.*

8. The Communication Ladder

Follow-up communication changes in tone as urgency increases, yet it must always stay grounded in respect. Each step of collection carries a different level of emphasis, but professionalism and empathy must remain constant. The Communication Ladder helps teams maintain consistency in tone, method, and intent, ensuring that firmness never turns into friction.

Collection Communication Ladder

Stage	Tone	Medium	Objective
Soft Reminder	Courteous and concise	Email or call	Create awareness, confirm receipt, and ensure visibility before a delay becomes routine.
Escalation	Firm and professional	Email and meeting	Gain commitment, secure a timeline, and raise visibility respectfully.

Stage	Tone	Medium	Objective
Finance Hold	Formal and contractual	Official letter	Drive action and accountability through policy enforcement with documentation and transparency

Golden Rule: Be firm on the issue, gentle with the person.

Consistency in tone preserves both cash flow and credibility. The goal is not only to collect payment but to earn respect that ensures the next one arrives without conflict.

> *Leadership Reflection: Tone is the invisible side of professionalism. Words may request payment, but tone earns trust.*

9. The Negotiation Mindset

Collections are not achieved through pressure. They are earned through composure and clarity. The most effective collectors are not loud. They are calm negotiators who guide clients toward payment as the natural next step.

Negotiation Mindset Tips: Securing Payments Without Losing Relationships

- **Focus on Interests, Not Positions:** Ask, "What is blocking approval?" instead of "Why have you not paid?" Understanding the reason opens doors that confrontation closes.

- **Use the Power of Pause:** After presenting facts, stay silent. Professional silence invites reflection and often prompts honest responses.

- **Anchor in Agreement:** Refer to signed terms, not emotions. Facts shift the discussion from personal tension to mutual accountability.

119

- **Offer Win–Win Options:** Suggest partial or progressive payment clearance. Flexibility keeps the relationship intact while keeping cash flowing.

- **Close on Optimism:** End every interaction with "We value our continued cooperation." Optimism signals confidence and preserves respect even when payment is delayed.

In payment negotiation, tone is leverage and empathy is influence. When discussions stay anchored in facts and professionalism, clients choose to cooperate rather than comply.

> *Leadership Reflection: Negotiation is not persuasion. It is alignment. The calm voice that secures payment today earns the trust that wins the next contract.*

10. Case: The Calm Negotiator

During a mechanical overhaul project, the client's finance department delayed payment, citing a budget rollover. Instead of escalating the issue through a series of emails, the project manager requested a short meeting to review the client's ledger together.

Within minutes, they discovered a small mismatch in the invoice reference. It was a clerical error, not a budget issue. The correction was made on the spot, and payment cleared within forty-eight hours.

Lesson: Calmness converts faster than pressure. Negotiation is not confrontation. It is patience backed by preparation. The right tone and the right facts often succeed where persistence alone fails.

> *Leadership Reflection: Clarity is the highest form of confidence. When professionals replace emotion with evidence, even a delay becomes an opportunity to strengthen trust.*

11. Analytical Dashboard: DSO and Collection Ratio

Cash performance must be measured as carefully as production output. An organization that tracks its cash metrics with the same precision as its operations never faces surprises. It anticipates them.

Key Collection Metrics

Metric	Formula	Ideal Target	Purpose
Days Sales Outstanding (DSO)	(Receivables / Average Daily Sales)	≤ 60 days	Indicates how fast revenue turns into cash.
Collection Ratio	(Collected / Due) × 100	≥ 90 %	Measures the effectiveness and consistency of follow-up.
>90 Days Ratio	(Invoices > 90 days / Total Receivables) × 100	≤ 10 %	Reveals chronic payment delays and potential credit risk.
Retention Recovery Rate	(Retention Collected / Retention Due) × 100	≥ 85 %	Evaluates closure discipline for long-term projects.

Trend Insight

Reducing DSO from 75 to 62 days while improving the collection ratio from 84% to 93% can unlock significant cash flow. That gain alone can finance growth without external borrowing. Every 10 day reduction in DSO acts as a hidden profit generator achieved through rhythm, not new revenue.

> **Leadership Reflection:** *What gets measured improves. Financial discipline grows when cash performance receives the same attention as operational output.*

12. Case: The Escalation That Recovered Millions

A petrochemical client withheld two major invoices, explaining that payments were delayed due to an internal budget review. After several polite reminders brought no progress, the project manager initiated a structured escalation that balanced respect with resolve.

A formal notice was issued under the Finance Hold Policy, temporarily pausing new site deployment until outstanding dues were cleared. Within 72 hours, the client released a partial settlement, and full payment followed within 2 weeks.

Lesson: Escalation carried out with respect turns negotiation into resolution. It was not aggression that made the difference, but clarity, consistency, and control. Respect gains attention faster than repetition, and process-backed firmness keeps that attention until closure.

> **Leadership Reflection:** *Professional firmness is not conflict. It is credibility in motion. When escalation follows process instead of emotion, it earns both payment and respect.*

13. Continuous Learning from Receivable Patterns

Collection data reveals more than just numbers. It reflects the overall health of a process. Every overdue entry tells a story of missing documents, unclear scope, or delayed coordination. Quarterly reviews of receivables should focus not only on totals but also on patterns and root causes.

Key Review Insights

- **Repetitive Reasons for Delay:** Identify recurring issues such as documentation gaps, client approval delays, or mismatched purchase orders.

- **Client Payment Patterns:** Separate habitual late payers from consistently prompt ones. This helps teams prioritise effort and forecast cash flow with greater accuracy.

- **Internal Response Times:** Track how quickly teams act on overdue alerts or client queries. Often, the speed of internal response defines the speed of collection.

Each insight should lead to a preventive improvement that closes the feedback loop between Finance, Operations, and Management. When receivable analysis becomes a routine practice, improvement becomes second nature.

> **Leadership Reflection:** *Data does more than show what happened. It points to where you can improve. Organisations that study their receivables carefully rarely face the same delay twice.*

14. Cultural Integration: Making Collection a Collective Habit

A process-driven organisation treats payment collection as everyone's responsibility, not the finance department's burden. When cash flow discipline becomes part of daily behaviour, the company moves from financial control to financial culture.

Cultural Practices That Build Collection Discipline

- **Integrate Collection KPIs into Scorecards:** Include DSO, on-time billing percentage, and overdue ratio in project and departmental performance metrics. What gets measured collectively gets managed consistently.

- **Celebrate On-Time Payments Publicly:** Acknowledge teams that achieve timely collections. Recognition

123

reinforces the belief that inflow efficiency is just as important as execution excellence.

- **Train Non-Finance Teams in Communication & Escalation Awareness:** Equip engineers, operations, and sales staff with a basic understanding of payment tone, escalation etiquette, and documentation requirements.

When every employee values inflow discipline, cash flow becomes a cultural reflex rather than a departmental chase. This mindset transforms the company's identity from chasing payments to earning trust.

> **Leadership Reflection:** *Cash flow is a reflection of culture. When teams take ownership of outcomes, finance stops chasing and leadership starts predicting.*

15. Case: The Client Who Respected Process

An industrial services firm introduced a secure online dashboard that displayed each client's own invoice ageing summary. Access was limited so that every client could view only their respective data and not the details of others.

For the first time, clients could clearly identify where their own internal approval delays were happening.

One senior procurement officer remarked, "This is the first contractor who made our process visible."

The result was immediate. Payment approvals doubled in speed, and disputes about missing documents or pending approvals disappeared.

Lesson: Transparency earns cooperation. When communication is guided by shared data instead of reminders, confrontation turns into collaboration. Visibility does not expose weakness, it builds mutual accountability.

> *Leadership Reflection: Process transparency builds trust faster than persuasion. When clients can see the truth, they stop resisting it.*

16. From Follow-Up to Financial Foresight

When receivables are tracked, analysed, and closed systematically, the finance team gains the ability to forecast cash inflows with accuracy. This foresight transforms collection from a reactive chase into a predictive management tool.

Accurate cash forecasting allows leaders to plan purchases, payroll, and investments with confidence, removing the need for last-minute borrowing and reactive decisions. It shifts finance from being a recorder of transactions to becoming a strategic enabler of growth.

Financial integration begins with follow-up precision. The same discipline that ensures timely collection also powers dashboards, forecasts, and financial intelligence. When every payment is tracked, verified, and learned from, cash flow stops fluctuating and starts performing.

> *Leadership Reflection: Follow-up is control, and foresight is leadership. When data turns into prediction, finance stops waiting for clarity and starts creating it.*

17. Insight: The Proof of a Process

When payments arrive on time, they validate the entire value chain, from sales negotiation and estimation accuracy to operational discipline and invoicing precision. A flawless process is not measured by how quickly teams work but by how predictably cash arrives.

Every timely payment is a silent audit that proves alignment, communication, and control have worked exactly as designed.

Cash is not the end of the process. It is the proof that the process worked.

> **Leadership Reflection:** *Money does not confirm success, consistency does. When cash flow becomes predictable, it signals not only profit but process maturity.*

Chapter 9: Finance Integration & Reporting

AG Business Flow Framework™

"Numbers tell stories only when processes speak the same language."

1. Introduction: From Accounting to Intelligence

Finance is no longer a back-office function. It is the analytical nerve centre of a process-driven organisation. In a world of multi-project operations, profitability depends not only on execution efficiency but also on how quickly financial insight is converted into action.

When finance works in harmony with estimation, operations, and billing, the organisation gains more than figures. It gains visibility, predictability, and foresight. This integration signals the beginning of Phase 5: Predictive Maturity, where systems no longer just report performance but begin to anticipate it.

An integrated finance function does not merely record results. It learns from them, turning every invoice, variance, and KPI into a continuous loop of intelligence that refines decisions and strengthens foresight.

> *Leadership Reflection: The most advanced finance systems do not count transactions, they teach organisations how to think.*

2. The Role of Finance as an Intelligence Hub

In earlier phases of the AG Business Flow Framework, finance safeguarded accuracy and accountability. Now it evolves into an intelligence hub that transforms raw operational data into strategic, real-time insight.

Integrated Role Across the Lifecycle

Lifecycle Stage	Finance Role	Key Outcome
Estimation	Validates pricing logic, cash flow assumptions, and risk exposure.	Builds confidence in bid accuracy.
Execution	Monitors cost burn, project margins, and cash exposure.	Prevents overrun and enhances visibility.
Billing	Tracks DSO and ensures timely collection of receivables.	Improves liquidity and forecast reliability.
Closure	Measures profitability, retention recovery, and variance feedback to estimation.	Strengthens future bids and cost models.

When fully integrated, finance stops being the end of the line and becomes the line of sight. It connects every process, project, and decision into one synchronised view of organisational truth.

> *Leadership Reflection: Finance integration does not create control, it reveals it. When every department's data speaks in harmony, leadership hears clarity, not noise.*

3. Building the Analytics Foundation

For finance to function as an intelligence system, it needs more than reports. It requires structure. Three key enablers form the backbone of financial analytics maturity.

Unified Data Architecture:

All departments, including Estimation, Operations, QA/QC, and Finance, must feed standardised cost, schedule, and progress data into a single ERP environment. This ensures that every number across the organisation speaks the same language, removing version conflicts and eliminating manual reconciliation.

Defined Performance Metrics:

Each department contributes measurable KPIs that link directly to financial outcomes. Productivity influences cost, risk influences margin, and schedule influences cash flow. Unified metrics convert departmental data into enterprise intelligence.

Visualization Layer:

Dashboards translate complex financial data into clear, actionable insights that are accessible to both executives and engineers. Visual management turns static information into real-time decision signals.

Together, these three elements form the organisation's performance cockpit, a single control centre where every action is measurable, every deviation visible, and every decision guided by data.

> **Leadership Reflection:** *Intelligence does not live in the data itself. It lives in the connections between them. When systems communicate clearly, leaders no longer search for clarity, they act on it.*

4. Key KPIs Defining Financial Intelligence

In a predictive organisation, finance is not measured by numbers alone. It is measured by insight. The following four KPIs form the heartbeat of financial intelligence, guiding leaders from visibility to foresight.

Core Predictive Finance KPIs

KPI	Definition	Healthy Benchmark	Decision Impact
Days Sales Outstanding (DSO)	The average number of days required to collect client payments.	40–55 days	Indicates liquidity strength and client discipline. A rising DSO highlights tighter cash conditions and potential credit exposure.
Work-in-Progress (WIP) Ageing	The age of unbilled executed work (0–30 / 31–60 / 61–90+ days).	Less than 15% above 60 days	Reflects billing discipline and operational momentum. High WIP ageing reveals process bottlenecks that restrict billing velocity.
Profit per Project (PPP)	(Revenue – Cost) / Revenue × 100	15% or higher for service-based firms	Measures true project success beyond completion and exposes the efficiency of cost control and scope management.
Process Health Index (PHI)	A composite score that combines process compliance, data accuracy, and timeliness on a 0–100 scale.	85 or above indicates stability	Represents process maturity and the financial quality of operational discipline. A falling PHI warns of data integrity issues before cost variance

> **Leadership Reflection:** *Financial strength is not created by numbers but by the discipline behind them. When KPIs are viewed as early signals rather than afterthoughts, finance evolves from reporting to predicting.*

5. The Process Health Index (PHI): From Concept to Capability

In the AG Business Flow Framework™, the Process Health Index (PHI) represents the financial pulse of operational discipline. It bridges the gap between process compliance and financial reliability, converting qualitative behaviours into measurable intelligence.

At its core, PHI answers one simple but decisive question: Can we trust the process behind our numbers?

The Concept Overview

At its simplest level:

PHI = (Timeliness × Accuracy × Documentation Integrity) / 100

- **Timeliness:** Were expenses, timesheets, and invoices entered on time?
- **Accuracy:** Were cost codes, quantities, and taxes correct?
- **Documentation Integrity:** Were SES, PO, and WCC approvals attached, signed, and traceable?

Each department's PHI contributes to the organisation's overall process health score. When PHI stays above 85, financial data can be trusted for predictive analysis. When it drops below 70, leadership must review process reliability before making major decisions.

This concept evolves into a multi-dimensional PHI Framework that aligns metrics, weights, and inter-departmental consistency into a single composite index.

PHI Calculation Framework

The PHI aggregates measurable attributes across five categories, converting them into a unified score from 0 to 100.

Category	Indicator Example	Measurement Source	Weight
Data Accuracy	% of entries without correction or rework	ERP / QA Logs	25%
Timeliness	% of tasks or reports completed within deadline	Schedule Tracker	20%
Compliance	Audit pass rate for documentation & approvals	Internal Audit / QA	20%
Variance Control	Deviation between plan vs. actual (cost/time ≤ ±10%)	Project Dashboard	20%
Cross-Department Sync	% of consistent shared data across departments	ERP Integration Audit	15%

Formula Example:

PHI = (A×0.25) + (T×0.20) + (C×0.20) + (V×0.20) + (S×0.15)

Where:

- A = Data Accuracy %
- T = Timeliness %
- C = Compliance %
- V = Variance Control %
- S = Sync Score %

Each metric is scored between 0 and 100 using ERP data, audits, and cross-department reports. The weighted total forms the organisation's overall Process Health Index.

PHI Interpretation and Leadership Response

PHI Range	Interpretation	Leadership Action
PHI Range	Interpretation	Leadership Action
90–100 (Excellent)	Highly reliable process environment. Predictive finance achievable.	Maintain benchmark and use as training reference.
80–89 (Stable)	Process under control with minor gaps.	Monitor trends quarterly.
70–79 (At Risk)	Delays or data inconsistencies emerging.	Initiate focused audits and process workshops.

Applying PHI in Dashboards

- **Trend Analysis:** Track PHI monthly by project or department to detect early weakness before it affects profitability.
- **Correlation:** Compare PHI with DSO, WIP Ageing, and PPP to see how operational discipline shapes financial performance.
- **Predictive Alerts:** Automate notifications when PHI falls below 80 to prompt early corrective action.

Example Scenario

If a project records:

- Data Accuracy = 90%
- Timeliness = 85%
- Compliance = 80%
- Variance Control = 88%
- Cross-Department Sync = 70%

Then:

PHI = (90×0.25) + (85×0.20) + (80×0.20) + (88×0.20) + (70×0.15)
= 83.9

Interpretation: The process is stable overall but shows early warning signs in cross-department synchronisation. Corrective alignment should occur before it affects billing or cost accuracy.

Strategic Significance

- A rising PHI signals increasing predictability and confidence in process control.

- A falling PHI often precedes cash delays, data conflicts, or audit observations.

- Sustaining PHI above 85 ensures finance, operations, and estimation speak one shared language, the mark of Phase 5 Predictive Maturity.

Leadership Reflection: The Process Health Index measures the strength of truth in numbers. When PHI is high, leaders can act decisively without doubting their data. That is the real return on process discipline.

Transformation Summary

From	To
Measuring outcomes	Measuring reliability of the process behind outcomes
Departmental data silos	Unified cross-functional data intelligence
Reactive reporting	Predictive visibility and proactive control
Accounting discipline	Decision-making confidence

Narrative Continuity

This integrated structure naturally flows from:

- Core KPIs (foundation of insight)

- PHI Concept (definition and purpose)
- PHI Framework (structure and formula)
- PHI Application (interpretation and dashboard use)
- Strategic Reflection (leadership foresight)

Together, these elements form a clear journey from metrics to maturity, which is precisely what Phase 5 represents.

> *Leadership Reflection:* Predictive finance is not about reacting faster, it is about seeing sooner. When every KPI tells a connected story, finance stops explaining the past and starts forecasting the future.

6. Dashboard Narrative: The "Finance Intelligence Console"

The Finance Intelligence Console is the digital face of Phase 5: Predictive Maturity. It is not a report. It is a real-time command centre that connects Operations, Estimation, and Finance under one unified lens. This console turns data into decisions, linking process performance with financial predictability.

Executive Dashboard (C-Suite View)

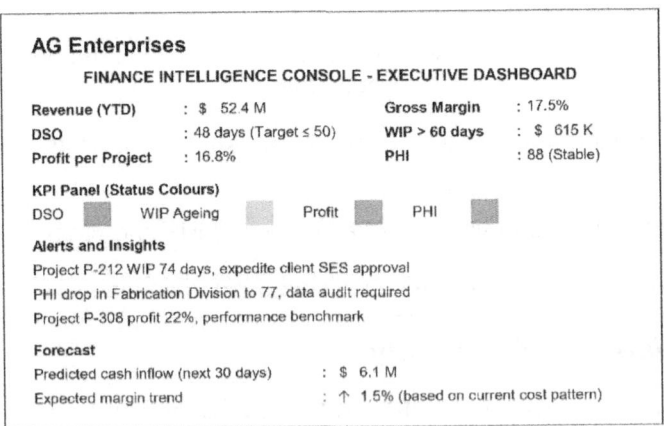

Figure 7 - Executive Dashboard

Purpose: At the executive level, the console converts complex KPIs into a strategic map of performance. Leaders no longer interpret spreadsheets. They see real-time financial intelligence supported by predictive analytics and early alerts.

Operational Dashboard (Department View)

AG Enterprises

PROJECT FINANCE SNAPSHOT - OPERATIONS INTERFACE

Project	Cost Utilization	Billing Status	PHI	DSO
P-212	87%	Pending SES	77	68d
P-308	74%	On Schedule	91	43d
P-411	80%	Client Review	86	54d

Figure 8 - Operational Dashboard

Insight: PHI correlates with billing efficiency. Higher PHI values consistently align with lower DSO. Operations now view Finance as feedback, not as audit.

Purpose: The operational dashboard transforms financial data into process feedback. Departments see causes such as delays, documentation quality, and data accuracy rather than just outcomes. This shift changes perception: Finance becomes a partner in performance rather than a post-event reviewer.

Interpretation

The Finance Intelligence Console demonstrates visibility combined with accountability.

- Executives view results: DSO, profit, PHI, and WIP trends.
- Departments view reasons: data quality, workflow timeliness, and process synchronization.

136

This dual-view structure turns finance from a reactive reviewer into a shared performance compass, aligning leadership vision with operational reality.

> **Leadership Reflection:** *A dashboard is not a mirror. It is a steering wheel. When everyone can see performance in real time, control becomes collective and improvement becomes instinctive.*

7. Case Example: Reporting Cycle Reduced by 50 %

Background

A diversified engineering company once took twelve days to close its monthly financials. Data from several divisions had to be gathered, verified, and consolidated manually, which caused delays, inconsistencies, and reactive decisions.

Action Plan

- **ERP Integration:** Unified Estimation, Execution, and Billing modules within a single ERP environment to enable live data flow.

- **Real-Time Dashboards:** Implemented Power BI performance consoles tracking key metrics such as DSO, WIP Ageing, PHI, and Profit per Project.

- **Weekly Digital Reviews:** Replaced static monthly summaries with weekly, finance-led sessions focused on trends, variances, and early intervention.

Results

- Reporting cycle reduced from 12 to 6 days (↓ 50 %).

- DSO improved from 67 to 44 days.

- PHI increased from 72 to 88, showing stronger documentation and data accuracy.

- Teams began resolving cost and billing anomalies proactively rather than post-review.

Impact

Finance evolved from a reporting department into a performance-intelligence hub. It no longer explained results, it predicted them. Executives gained real-time visibility, and decision cycles accelerated across the organisation.

> **Leadership Reflection:** *Integration does not shorten reports, it shortens uncertainty. When information moves instantly, leadership moves intelligently.*

8. Data Visualization & Predictive Decision-Making

Visualization is not decoration, it is decision acceleration. A well-built dashboard transforms finance from static reporting into continuous awareness, turning numbers into stories and insights into anticipation.

From Data to Foresight

- A red WIP trend line highlights unbilled work and prompts early invoicing, preventing cash from sitting idle.
- A declining PHI exposes process inconsistencies before they turn into audit remarks or client disputes.
- Trend overlays show how strong documentation discipline consistently leads to faster collections and lower DSO.

Predictive Simulation

Modern dashboards do more than display data. They simulate possible outcomes. Finance teams can now explore scenarios before results occur.

For example: if PHI improves by just five points, DSO may drop by four days, releasing roughly 1.2 million USD in cash flow.

This link between process health and financial velocity gives leaders the power to act early rather than react later.

The New Language of Performance Intelligence

In a mature organization, data no longer waits to be interpreted. It speaks, connects, and anticipates. Visualization becomes the bridge between numbers and narrative, between awareness and action. Leaders stop waiting for monthly summaries because real-time intelligence already guides their decisions.

> *Leadership Reflection: A dashboard that predicts has greater value than one that merely reports. Insight creates understanding, but foresight creates leadership.*

9. Linking Financial Intelligence to Operational Decisions

The real strength of integration appears when financial intelligence begins to shape decisions in real time. At that point, data is no longer a record of the past, it becomes a management instrument that guides action in the present.

Strategic Impact

- **Margin Forecasting:** Connects cost behaviour with future profitability, allowing proactive margin protection instead of late correction.
- **Client Risk Profiling:** Tracks DSO and WIP patterns to identify clients whose payment habits pose a potential cash-flow risk.
- **Bid Strategy:** Uses historical Profit-per-Project data to refine pricing and strengthen bidding accuracy for upcoming opportunities.

Operational Impact

- **Cash-Flow Prioritization:** Procurement and resource allocation are planned in line with projected client inflows, ensuring liquidity and operational stability.

- **Process Quality:** PHI trends pinpoint where retraining or tighter controls are needed before small issues turn into financial deviation.

- **Performance Accountability:** Each project team owns its financial and process KPIs, creating a direct connection between field execution and fiscal outcomes.

Organizational Impact

When this level of integration takes hold, finance stops functioning as a separate department and becomes a shared discipline. Every manager begins to read financial dashboards the same way they read schedules, as part of their everyday language of performance. The result is not only stronger reporting but also an organisation where strategy, execution, and finance operate as one synchronised system.

> *Leadership Reflection: Integration is not about systems connecting, it is about people aligning. When every team understands the numbers behind their work, decisions stop being reactive and start becoming responsible.*

10. Best Practices for Building a Finance Intelligence System

Creating a Finance Intelligence System is not a technology project. It is a transformation in visibility and behaviour. The following practices turn data integration into foresight and daily discipline.

Core Best Practices

- **Centralized ERP Integration:** Combine Estimation, Procurement, and Execution under one shared data structure to remove silos and maintain real-time accuracy.

- **Standard Cost Coding & Templates:** Apply consistent cost structures and reporting formats across departments so that analytics reflect true comparisons.

- **Automated Alerts & Exceptions:** Set up instant notifications for PHI drops, DSO breaches, or cost overruns. This allows proactive correction before variance widens.

- **Role-Based Dashboards:** Design dashboards according to user roles. Executives focus on profitability and long-term trends, while engineers monitor process accuracy and resource efficiency.

- **Monthly Predictive Review Meetings:** Replace backward-looking reviews with sessions focused on trends, forecasts, and early risk signals.

- **AI-Assisted Forecasting:** Use predictive models to forecast cash-flow changes and cost variations before they occur, enabling early action and better control.

- **Process Audits Based on PHI:** Use the Process Health Index to identify areas where process reliability is falling and direct audit effort where control is most needed.

- **Cross-Functional Literacy:** Train every department to read KPIs and understand how their work influences financial results. When everyone speaks the language of numbers, finance becomes shared accountability.

These practices transform finance from a recording function into a living intelligence system that helps every level of the organisation act before problems appear.

> *Leadership Reflection:* Technology may enable intelligence, but culture sustains it. The strength of a finance system is not defined by how advanced its dashboards are, but by how naturally people use them to think, decide, and improve.

11. Process Health and Financial Culture

A financially mature organisation does not just manage numbers, it manages behaviour through numbers. When metrics such as PHI, DSO, and Profit per Project become part of everyday conversations, teams begin to see that financial health is simply a reflection of process discipline.

Behaviour Reflected in Metrics

- A delayed PO does not only slow procurement, it also disrupts cash flow.

- A missing SES does not only delay invoicing, it also blocks revenue recognition.

- A low PHI score does not only indicate weak data, it also signals a decline in organisational credibility.

The Cultural Shift

Finance, at this stage, is no longer a scoreboard. It becomes a mirror that reflects how well processes align and how responsibly teams execute. When people understand their financial fingerprint, accountability turns into a shared habit and improvement becomes second nature.

> **Leadership Reflection:** *Financial maturity is not achieved when finance controls the process. It is achieved when the process controls the finance. Numbers reveal the truth only when the culture tells the same story.*

12. Financial Leadership Insights

The shift from financial reporting to predictive intelligence calls for a new kind of leadership, one that reads numbers not as results, but as relationships between process and performance.

Mindset Shifts for Predictive Leaders

- **From Data to Dialogue:** Finance should speak in stories, not spreadsheets. True intelligence turns information into context that inspires action.

- **From Isolation to Integration:** Financial insight must flow across departments so that every decision reflects a shared understanding of impact.

- **From Accuracy to Agility:** Perfect numbers lose value if they arrive too late. Timely truth is always better than delayed precision.

- **From Control to Foresight:** Leadership is not about enforcing compliance through pressure. It is about shaping behaviour through understanding.

- **From Reporting to Storytelling:** The best financial leaders translate numbers into meaning, helping teams see why performance matters, not just how much.

Insight

When numbers and processes speak the same language, leadership gains fluency in foresight. Finance stops being the end of the story and becomes the lens through which the organisation learns, anticipates, and improves.

> **Leadership Reflection:** *Predictive finance begins with a simple belief. Numbers do not drive performance, people who understand them do.*

13. Conclusion

Finance Integration and Reporting marks the true turning point of the AG Business Flow Framework™. It is the stage where control matures into intelligence.

When DSO, WIP, Profit per Project, and PHI converge within one unified ecosystem, they reveal more than financial results. They uncover the behaviour of the organisation itself.

In a predictive enterprise, dashboards replace debates and numbers replace assumptions. Finance no longer serves as a mirror reflecting the past. It becomes a window that reveals the future.

As we move into Phase 5: Predictive Maturity, finance stands as the bridge between process and performance, where numbers stop simply accounting for work and begin to speak the language of leadership.

> **Closing Reflection:** *Financial clarity is not the end of the process. It is the beginning of foresight.*

Chapter 10: Digital Transformation - From Data to Discipline

AG Business Flow Framework™

"Digitalization is not IT, it's institutional intelligence."

1. Introduction: The Turning Point to Predictive Maturity

Every organisation eventually reaches a defining crossroads, the point where manual control can go no further. Beyond that threshold lies predictive maturity, a stage where data no longer records what happened but begins to guide what should happen next.

For AG Enterprises, this turning point came not because systems failed but because people outgrew them. The company had already mastered process integrity, with estimation, billing, and finance working in harmony. Yet decisions still relied on scattered reports, personal memory, and isolated departmental data.

It was not inefficiency that held progress back. It was invisibility. And the answer was not more effort but greater digital clarity.

> *"We didn't go digital to look modern. We did it to see clearly."*
>
> *Managing Director, AG Enterprises*

This chapter marks the pivotal moment in the AG Business Flow Framework™. It is the shift from operational integrity to digital intelligence and from process-driven performance to data-driven leadership.

2. The Trigger: When Data Stopped Speaking the Same Language

The transformation began after a client progress review went off track. Operations reported 90% completion. Finance showed 75%. Procurement indicated that 30% of materials were still pending.

Every department was right, but only within its own data sheet. The company had multiple truths and no single version of them. That moment of contradiction became the catalyst for change.

AG Enterprises faced a simple but powerful realisation: without integration, even accurate departments can create an inaccurate organisation.

The journey toward predictive maturity did not start in the IT room. It began in the boardroom, with a leadership decision to unify data, processes, and people under one shared language of truth.

3. The Essence of Digital Transformation

Digital transformation is not the installation of software. It is the redefinition of how work, information, and accountability move through an organisation. It changes not what people do, but how they think about doing it.

The journey evolves through four progressive stages of digital maturity:

- **Digitization:** Converting manual data into digital records and creating the foundation for visibility.
- **Digitalization:** Automating repetitive tasks to build consistency and remove human bottlenecks.
- **Integration:** Connecting all functions into one intelligent ecosystem that delivers a single version of operational truth.

- **Intelligence:** Using analytics and predictive insights to anticipate outcomes instead of reacting to them.

The highest form of transformation is not automation. It is awareness. An organisation becomes truly digital when everyone, from the technician to the CFO, sees the same truth at the same time.

> *Leadership Reflection: Technology alone does not transform organisations. Transparency does. Digital tools simply make it impossible to ignore the truth.*

4. The Pillars of Predictive Maturity

Predictive maturity depends not on technology alone, but on the balance of leadership, structure, and culture. Each pillar strengthens the others, creating a sustainable ecosystem of digital intelligence.

Pillar	Purpose	Outcome
Leadership Vision	Drive transformation from the top.	Unified direction and digital accountability.
Process Standardisation	Build structure before automation.	Consistent workflows and predictable results across all departments.
People and Culture	Ensure adoption through ownership, not enforcement.	Sustained behavioural change and long-term engagement.
Technology Infrastructure	Connect systems, ensure scalability, and maintain secure integrations.	A single, connected ecosystem of operational truth.

Pillar	Purpose	Outcome
Data Governance	Maintain accuracy, integrity, and reliability across all information flows.	Trusted, auditable decision-making.
Continuous Improvement	Institutionalise learning through review and reflection.	Ongoing evolution and innovation at every level.

Together, these six pillars turn digitalisation from a project into a philosophy that aligns people, processes, and technology around one shared truth.

> **Leadership Reflection:** *Digital maturity is not defined by having the latest tools. It is defined by having the clearest direction. When these pillars stand firm, transformation stops being an event and becomes a habit.*

5. Transformation Stories: The Systems That Changed the Culture

Case 1: Barcode Tracking - From Manual Entry to Real-Time Precision

Before: Workshop job cards were handwritten and time entries were compiled manually hours later, often from memory. This created discrepancies in job costing, payroll, and billing.

Challenge:

- Reporting lag: 48 hours
- Job-cost accuracy: below 70%
- Limited visibility across ongoing activities

Transformation: A barcode-based job tracking system connected engineers, jobs, and activities through mobile scanning. Each scan updated Google Sheets and the ERP system in real time, feeding a live productivity dashboard.

After:

- Job-cost accuracy improved from 68% to 92%
- Payroll reconciliation time reduced from 2 days to 30 minutes
- Overall reporting time cut by 50%
- Supervisors gained live visibility into productivity

Cultural Impact: Transparency replaced supervision. Engineers began competing not for recognition but for self-improvement. They no longer waited for instructions but tracked their own progress.

> **Leadership Reflection:** *Technology did not enforce accountability, it revealed it. When people can see their performance in real time, discipline becomes instinct rather than instruction.*

Case 2: ERP Integration - One Source of Truth

Before: Departments operated independently. Estimation relied on Excel. Procurement depended on email approvals. Finance maintained ledgers manually. Every decision required multiple verification loops and reconciliation steps.

Challenge:

- No unified data flow between departments
- Duplicate POs and manual cost-tracking errors
- Reactive planning caused by fragmented visibility

Transformation: Implementation of Microsoft Dynamics ERP unified Estimation, Procurement, Operations, HR, and Finance under a single platform. Material requests, purchase approvals, and cost allocations became automated, auditable, and instantly traceable.

After:

- Purchase cycle time reduced from 7 days to 3 days
- Duplicate POs eliminated (0%)
- Real-time job-cost visibility enabled same-day financial reporting
- Financial reconciliation accuracy improved to 99.5%

Result: Visibility across the value chain improved, increasing profitability per project by 8%. That improvement was equal to adding one extra project per year, achieved entirely through process efficiency.

Cultural Impact: Meetings no longer revolved around "who is right." Instead, teams began asking "what is next." Discussions shifted from justification to judgment and from defending numbers to directing action.

> **Leadership Reflection:** *Integration does not remove accountability, it reveals alignment. When everyone works from one truth, energy shifts from correction to creation.*

Case 3: BI Dashboards - From Reports to Real-Time Intelligence

Before: Every Friday, engineers spent hours preparing manual Excel reports for management. By the time data was compiled, decisions were already outdated.

Challenge:

- Reactive management and delayed visibility
- Inconsistent reporting formats across departments

- Excessive time spent compiling, verifying, and reconciling data

Transformation: Power BI dashboards were integrated to pull live data directly from the ERP and barcode tracking systems. Executives could now monitor estimation turnaround, project margins, resource utilisation, and cash exposure in real time.

After:

- Report preparation time reduced from 6 hours to 2 hours
- Management review duration reduced by 30%
- Early deviation alerts lowered margin leakage from 7% to 1–2%
- On-time client reporting improved by 45%

Strategic Impact: Dashboards transformed management reviews into live, data-driven discussions. Executives began using these dashboards during client meetings, turning transparency into a competitive advantage.

> **Leadership Reflection:** *Real-time intelligence does not just accelerate decisions, it builds trust. When leaders see the same truth as their teams and clients, credibility becomes the organisation's strongest currency.*

6. Measurable Outcomes of Transformation

Digital transformation at AG Enterprises delivered measurable results across every stage of the business, from estimation precision to financial accuracy and client responsiveness.

KPI	Before	After	Improvement
Quotation Turnaround	5.2 days	3.0 days	↓ 42%
Job Cost Accuracy	65%	88%	↑ 35%

KPI	Before	After	Improvement
Purchase Cycle Time	7 days	3 days	↓ 57%
Payroll Processing	16 hrs/month	2 hrs/month	↓ 87%
Customer Response Time	48 hrs	12 hrs	↓ 75%
Margin Leakage	5–7%	1–2%	70% reduction

Interpretation

Digitalisation at AG Enterprises proved that transformation is not about speed alone. It is about clarity, consistency, and control. When processes, data, and people operate within a single system of truth, efficiency becomes the natural outcome of transparency.

> **Leadership Reflection:** *Numbers improve only after visibility improves. Digital transformation does not replace discipline, it amplifies it.*

7. Managing Change: Where Technology Meets Behaviour

Technology may ignite transformation, but behaviour sustains it. AG Enterprises understood that systems would only succeed if the people using them trusted the purpose behind them. The real challenge was not coding, it was conviction.

Change Management Strategies

- **Involve, Don't Impose:** Employees co-designed workflows, creating ownership and reducing resistance.
- **Digital Champions Network:** Internal mentors and early adopters became advocates who helped peers navigate new tools.

- **Transparent Communication:** Town-hall sessions clarified that digitalisation was introduced for accuracy, not surveillance.

- **Continuous Learning:** "Friday Fix" sessions focused on one feature at a time, making change manageable and habitual.

- **Recognition Culture:** Teams who eliminated manual work were recognised publicly, turning efficiency into pride.

"Once we saw our data in real time, we didn't want to go back."

Project Lead, AG Enterprises

Within four months, system adoption grew from 40% to 92%. One senior technician, initially sceptical, became a digital mentor who used his real-time performance dashboard to train juniors and improve shop-floor efficiency.

Leadership Insight

Digital transformation succeeds when people see progress, not pressure. When tools empower rather than evaluate, technology stops being an obligation and becomes a source of pride.

> **Leadership Reflection:** *Change does not happen when tools arrive, it happens when trust does.*

8. Digital Readiness Checklist

Before any digital transformation begins, leaders must assess not the software but the system of readiness that surrounds it. Transformation succeeds only when the organisation is prepared to change as quickly as its technology.

Readiness Dimensions

- **Strategic Readiness:** Are workflows standardised, documented, and consistently followed?

- **Process Readiness:** Are workflows standardised, documented, and consistently followed?

- **People Readiness:** Are change champions identified, empowered, and trained?

- **Technology Readiness:** Are systems integrated, scalable, and secure?

- **Data Readiness:** Is information clean, validated, backed up, and traceable?

- **Cultural Readiness:** Does the organisation value transparency, learning, and accountability?

If the answer is "yes" to at least 70% of these dimensions, the organisation is ready to begin digital transformation. If not, the journey must start with alignment, not automation.

> *Leadership Reflection: Digital transformation begins with readiness, not resources. A clear and aligned culture is the only foundation that technology can truly stand on.*

9. Sustaining Predictive Maturity

Digitalisation is not a project, it is a continuous cycle of learning and refinement. Predictive maturity is sustained not through technology updates but through an organisation's discipline to keep improving its digital behaviour.

AG Enterprises maintains its momentum through the following recurring practices:

- **Monthly Digital Health Reviews:** Cross-functional teams review KPI dashboards together, tracking DSO, PHI, utilisation, and workflow efficiency.

- **Quarterly Improvement Meetings:** End users propose system enhancements and process refinements to ensure that innovation remains user-led.

- **Annual Integration Projects:** The ERP ecosystem expands each year by incorporating IoT data streams, AI-driven analytics, and new automation layers.

- **Training Refresh Weeks:** Regular training cycles renew digital literacy, reinforce process awareness, and encourage innovation at every level.

Applied Example: ERP Ecosystem Evolution in Practice

When we say "The ERP ecosystem expands each year by incorporating IoT data streams, AI-driven analytics, and new automation layers," it means the organisation is not freezing its digital system at the ERP level but continuously layering new technologies that extend insight, automation, and foresight.

Example 1: IoT Data Streams - Visibility from the Shop Floor

Scenario: Machines on the workshop floor such as CNC lathes, pumps, compressors, or coating booths are fitted with IoT sensors.

Integration:

- Sensors send data (temperature, vibration, uptime, load hours) directly to the ERP system.
- Dashboards display real-time utilisation, downtime, and maintenance.

Impact:

- Maintenance becomes predictive as repairs are scheduled before failure.
- Productivity reports update automatically with no manual entries needed.
- Equipment uptime improves from 92% to 98%.

Example 2: AI-Driven Analytics - Predicting Cost and Cash-Flow Trends

Scenario: The ERP holds large datasets including estimates, project costs, invoice dates, DSO patterns, and PHI scores.

Integration:

- AI models analyse historical trends to forecast potential cost overruns, margin shifts, or cash delays.
- For example, the system predicts: "Client X's DSO may increase by 10 days next quarter based on prior trends and approval patterns."

Impact:

- Finance adjusts credit terms in advance.
- Management reallocates cash proactively.
- AI converts historical data into forward visibility.

Example 3: Automation Layers - From Entry to Action

Scenario: Previously, project engineers manually entered daily reports and job completions into ERP.

Integration:

- Using barcode scans and mobile apps, data now auto-updates in ERP.
- Smart workflows trigger next actions once a completion record is uploaded, and ERP automatically alerts Finance to generate an invoice draft.

Impact:

- Manual entry time reduced by 80 %.
- Billing accuracy improved to near 100 %.
- Human effort shifted from updating systems to analysing outcomes.

In Summary

Each year, the ERP gains new "eyes" through IoT sensors, new "intelligence" through AI analytics, and new "reflexes" through automation workflows. This evolution turns the system from a database into a digital organism that learns, anticipates, and adapts with every project.

> *Leadership Reflection: Digital maturity grows not by adding tools but by deepening visibility. Each integration layer transforms data from record-keeping into real-time foresight.*

10. Transformation Snapshot: 3 Systems, 9 Metrics, 1 Culture Shift

Digital transformation is not measured by how many tools an organisation installs, but by how many truths it unifies.

At AG Enterprises, the journey to predictive maturity was built on three core systems, governed by nine performance metrics, and culminating in one defining culture shift that moved the company from reporting performance to living it in real time.

The Three Systems That Changed Everything

- **Barcode Tracking System:** Connected field engineers, job cards, and productivity data to real-time dashboards.
- **ERP Integration (Microsoft Dynamics):** Unified estimation, procurement, HR, and finance into one connected ecosystem of truth.
- **Power BI Dashboards:** Turned raw data into live performance intelligence accessible to every level of leadership.

Together, these systems did more than automate processes. They orchestrated visibility and created a single shared language of performance.

The Nine Metrics That Measured Progress

Area	Initiative	Outcome
Workshop	Barcode Tracking	90 % less manual entry, Real-time job-cost accuracy
Organization	ERP Integration	Unified data, 8 % profitability increase
Leadership	Power BI Dashboards	65 % faster reporting, 70 % fewer delays

These initiatives collectively improved nine measurable KPIs, including:

- Quotation turnaround time
- Job-cost accuracy
- Purchase cycle time
- Payroll processing efficiency
- Customer response time
- Margin leakage
- DSO (Days Sales Outstanding)
- PHI (Process Health Index)
- On-time reporting rate

Each metric became more than a number. It became a behavioural mirror showing how closely every process aligned with truth.

The One Culture Shift

The greatest transformation was not technological, it was psychological.

- Decisions that once took days now happen within hours.
- Departments no longer argued over data, they acted on the same information.

- Teams stopped "submitting reports" and started living on dashboards.

For the first time, the organisation was not chasing accuracy, it was operating inside it.

> *Leadership Reflection: When three systems produce nine metrics that reshape one culture, transformation becomes irreversible. Technology may connect data, but only culture connects meaning.*

11. Key Lessons for Digital Culture

Digital transformation does not end when systems go live. It begins when mindsets go digital.

The experience of AG Enterprises shows that technology succeeds only when culture evolves with it. Each lesson represents a shift from tools to thinking, from digital adoption to digital behaviour.

Lessons for Sustaining a Digital Culture

- **Start with Why, Not Software.** Digital tools must serve a purpose, not prestige. The goal is clarity, not complexity.
- **Standardise Before You Automate.** Automating unclear workflows only multiplies confusion. Build structure before seeking speed.
- **Adoption Is the Real KPI.** A tool that is unused is a cost. A tool that is embraced is capital. Measure participation, not installation.
- **Celebrate the Small Wins.** Every saved minute and every reduced step builds trust in the transformation.
- **Data Integrity Is Leadership Integrity.** Numbers that cannot be trusted cannot be managed. Truth in data is the foundation of credibility.

- **Lead Digitally.** When leaders make decisions through dashboards, digital stops being a project and becomes culture.

- **Evolve Constantly.** Predictive maturity grows one insight at a time. It is sustained not by upgrades but by understanding.

Leadership Reflection: Digital culture is not born from technology. It is born from trust. When leaders model data-driven decision-making, transformation moves from system to spirit.

12. Conclusion: The Discipline Behind Intelligence

Digital transformation is not about IT. It is about institutional intelligence. It gives structure to experience, visibility to performance, and rhythm to decision-making.

The journey of AG Enterprises proves that transformation is not driven by technology alone. It is driven by discipline, accountability, and vision.

"Digital tools amplify discipline. They cannot replace it."

This moment marks the threshold of Phase 5, Predictive Maturity, where organisations no longer ask "What happened?" but "What happens next?"

And that is the true language of institutional intelligence.

Chapter 11: Case Study - AG Enterprises

AG Business Flow Framework™

"Transformation becomes measurable when data meets discipline."

1. Introduction: The Framework Comes Alive

Until now, each chapter has explored a principle of the AG Business Flow Framework from Lead Discipline to Digital Maturity. This chapter brings those principles to life.

AG Enterprises, a mid-sized industrial services company in the Gulf region, became the proving ground where process theory met operational reality. The framework was not simply implemented, it was lived every day.

What follows is not the story of software installation, but of alignment. It is the story of how Sales, Estimation, Execution, and Finance began to move together through measurable data, cultural ownership, and leadership vision.

> *"We didn't just automate forms. We built flow."*
>
> *Managing Director, AG Enterprises*

2. Phase 1: Lead Discipline - Recognizing the Pattern of Delay

Before: Sales operations relied on individual follow-ups and scattered email threads. Critical enquiries often slipped through unnoticed, and response times varied from person to person instead of following a defined system.

After Applying the AG Framework (Lead Discipline): A centralised enquiry tracker was introduced to map every opportunity through a clear five-stage funnel: Lead, Qualification, Estimation, Negotiation, and Award.

Weekly funnel review meetings replaced reactive chases with proactive coordination and shared accountability.

KPI Improvement Snapshot

KPI	Before	After	Gain
Response Time	5–6 days	2.5 days	↓ 58 %
Conversion Rate	28 %	44 %	+ 16 pts
Enquiry Traceability	Low	100 %	Full visibility

Insight: Lead discipline did not accelerate sales through pressure. It did so through visibility. By replacing memory with method, AG Enterprises built the foundation of predictability that every later phase relied on.

> *"I stopped searching mail archives. Now I search the funnel."*
>
> *Aman K., Sales Engineer*

3. Phase 2: Estimation Precision - Engineering Consistency

The next stage of the AG Business Flow Framework™ required more than speed. It demanded measurable precision. Estimation had to evolve from an individual skill into an organizational standard.

Before:

- Personal spreadsheets and subjective cost assumptions
- Inconsistent norms and margin interpretations
- No uniform review or validation process

After Applying the Framework (Estimation Precision):

- Standardized templates and benchmark libraries established
- Approval workflow introduced for review and risk assessment
- Historical data integrated to build cost intelligence over time

KPI Improvement Snapshot

KPI	Before	After	Change
Estimation Turnaround	4 days	1.5 days	↓ 62 %
Accuracy Variance	±18 %	±5 %	↑ 72 %
Win Rate	28 %	44 %	+16 pts

Leadership Lesson 1: Precision is not about speed. It is about verified repeatability. By turning estimation from intuition into analytics, AG Enterprises transformed credibility into a measurable advantage.

> *"Earlier our accuracy was intuition. Now it is evidence."*
>
> *Shazia M., Estimation Lead*

4. Phase 3: Execution Control - From Visibility to Predictability

The Execution Control phase of the AG Business Flow Framework™ came to life through barcode-based activity tracking that linked manpower, job cards, and work progress into real-time visibility. Execution was no longer guided by memory or supervision. It was measured and managed through data.

KPI Improvement Snapshot

KPI	Before	After	Change
Schedule Adherence	68 %	92 %	+24 pts
Rework Hours	12 %	4 %	↓ 67 %
Daily Progress Reporting	Manual	Automatic	Real-time

Team Reflection 1: Visibility builds calm. People perform better when facts replace speculation and when effort is guided by evidence instead of assumptions.

> *"Earlier I managed by noise. Now I manage by numbers."*
>
> *Shahul, Workshop Supervisor*

5. Phase 4: Financial Integrity - Closing the Loop

A recurring conflict between Operations and Finance revealed the missing link in the value chain. Billing accuracy was suffering because completion data arrived late and inconsistently.

The Financial Integrity phase of the AG Business Flow Framework™ introduced a digital handover gate that ensured no invoice could proceed without verified job closure. This single control converted confusion into collaboration.

KPI Improvement Snapshot

KPI	Before	After	Gain
Invoice Cycle	22 days	7 days	↓ 68 %
Billing Accuracy	87 %	98 %	+ 11 pts

KPI	Before	After	Gain
Invoice Rejections	1 in 5	1 in 20	↓ 75 %

Leadership Lesson 2: Integrity is the foundation of speed. Clean data moves faster than arguments. Financial integrity not only improved cash flow but also restored trust between departments and made every number defensible.

> *"Conflict ended when evidence began."*
>
> *Laila A., Finance Coordinator*

6. Phase 5: Predictive Maturity - Making Data Work for Decisions

By the fifth phase, AG Enterprises was operating through live, interconnected dashboards. Estimation accuracy, schedule adherence, billing performance, and DSO were visible to everyone, from workshop supervisors to the Managing Director. Data was no longer confined to departments. It had become organizational intelligence.

KPI Improvement Snapshot

KPI	Before	After	Improvement
Days Sales Outstanding (DSO)	82 days	54 days	↓ 34 %
Collection Efficiency	71 %	93 %	+ 22 pts
Monthly Cash Predictability	Low	High	Stable inflow

Result: Finance no longer reacted, it anticipated. Operations no longer guessed, they projected. Leaders stopped asking for reports because they could read the truth in real time.

Team Reflection 2: When data is shared, accountability stops feeling like surveillance and starts feeling like empowerment.

Leadership Lesson 3: Predictive maturity begins when data stops being information and starts becoming instinct. At this stage, performance is no longer tracked, it is anticipated.

7. Framework in Full View: Phase-by-Phase Impact

The five phases of the AG Business Flow Framework™ transformed AG Enterprises from a reactive operation into a predictive organization. Each phase strengthened the next, creating a seamless chain from visibility to foresight.

Phase-by-Phase Transformation Summary

Phase of AG Framework	Core Focus	Signature Metric Improvement
Lead Discipline	Enquiry Response	↓ 58 % response time
Estimation Precision	Cost Accuracy	↑ 72 %
Execution Control	Schedule Adherence	+24 pts
Financial Integrity	Billing Accuracy	+11 pts
Predictive Maturity	DSO Reduction	↓ 34 %

Cumulative Result

- Operational Cycle Time: ↓ 46 %
- Cash Conversion: ↑ 28 %
- Client Satisfaction: 9.1 / 10
- Employee Retention: 94 %

The framework did more than improve numbers. It built rhythm, reliability, and respect between teams, proving that true transformation begins when processes start thinking for themselves.

8. Five Key Success Factors

The transformation at AG Enterprises was not accidental. It was engineered through focus, rhythm, and reinforcement. Five consistent practices sustained momentum and turned digital change into a lasting cultural habit.

Leadership Visibility: Executives personally reviewed dashboards every week, ensuring that transformation remained a leadership priority and not just an IT initiative. When leaders watch the metrics, teams start watching their methods.

Pilot and Prove Method: Early wins in estimation and billing validated the framework's credibility and removed scepticism. Each success became a proof point that built confidence before wider implementation.

Unified Data Language: By standardizing processes across the ERP ecosystem, every department operated from one source of truth. Cross-department conflicts disappeared because facts, not opinions, guided discussions.

Continuous Upskilling: A network of Process Champions trained peers each month, turning early adopters into mentors. Upskilling was not an event, it became a steady rhythm of learning and improvement.

Recognition Culture: Teams that showed consistency and compliance were celebrated publicly. Awards recognised discipline over heroics, rewarding reliability rather than rescue.

9. Lessons for Leaders

Transformation begins with discomfort because pain reveals priority. At AG Enterprises, the willingness to confront inefficiency was the first real sign of maturity.

Process Precedes Platform: Document before digitizing. A flawed workflow does not become efficient simply because it is automated.

Data Breeds Trust: Transparency removes politics. When everyone sees the same truth, debate turns into direction.

Leaders Must Model Metrics: When executives review dashboards, teams learn to think in numbers instead of opinions. If the top checks the data, everyone else follows.

Celebrate Reliability, Not Rescue: Heroic recoveries may look impressive, but steady systems endure. Discipline, not drama, defines lasting transformation.

> *Leadership Reflection: Digital maturity does not begin with dashboards. It begins with courage. Leaders must first measure themselves before they can measure their teams.*

10. Lessons for Teams

Transformation succeeds when teams see metrics as allies, not audits. At AG Enterprises, empowerment came from realising that data is not control, it is confidence.

Own Your Numbers: They are not inspection but validation. When you own your data, you own your direction.

Ask for Clarity Early: Confusion grows over time. Questions asked on Day 1 save rework on Day 30.

Collaborate Across Boundaries. Information flow drives process flow. The more teams share, the fewer issues need escalation.

See Metrics as Mirrors. They reflect habits, not judgment. A metric is feedback and a daily chance to adjust before someone else needs to intervene.

Stay Curious. Continuous improvement is the oxygen of progress. Curiosity sustains innovation long after systems are established.

> **Team Reflection:** *A disciplined process does not restrict freedom. It creates it. When teams trust data, they stop waiting for direction and start moving with confidence.*

11. Cross-Functional Reflection

During an internal debrief, each department was asked a simple question: "What did transformation mean to you?" Their answers revealed that digital maturity was not just a process shift but a mindset evolution.

Department	Reflection
Department	Reflection
Sales	"Visibility made targets real. We stopped over-promising."
Estimation	"Consistency reduced anxiety. Accuracy is now our pride."
Operations	"We no longer firefight. We forecast."
Finance	"Collections became a team effort, not a blame game."

Insight: Every department found its own form of freedom within structure. What began as a process overhaul evolved into shared clarity and a culture where performance, trust, and purpose spoke the same language.

> **Leadership Reflection:** *When every function speaks through the same framework, alignment becomes automatic. Transformation, at its core, is not about tools but about truth made visible.*

12. Leadership Reflection

During the 2024 annual meet, the Managing Director summarised the transformation journey with simple clarity and depth:

"**The AG Business Flow Framework** did not change who we are. It revealed who we could be. Every metric was a mirror showing whether our values were real."

13. Lessons for Other Organizations

The transformation at AG Enterprises offered insights that extend far beyond one company. They form a roadmap for any organization seeking process-driven maturity.

Typical Challenge	AG Framework Response
Siloed Operations	Unified data dashboards connecting estimation, execution, and finance
Manual Decision-Making	Automated visibility with real-time dashboards replacing static reports
Late Billing and Cash Flow Issues	Financial Integrity Gate ensuring verified closure before invoicing
Skill Gaps in Adoption	Process Champions programme mentoring teams through transition
Leadership Detachment	Weekly KPI reviews led by executives, embedding accountability at the top

Actionable Takeaway: Start small. Identify one measurable weakness, apply the AG Flow discipline, and scale success step by step. Clarity builds confidence, and credibility grows where consistency lives.

> *Leadership Reflection: Digital transformation is not imitation. It is adaptation. Every organization has its own flow, and the real challenge is to make that flow visible, measurable, and repeatable.*

14. Conclusion: Alignment Over Perfection

Eighteen months after its first pilot, AG Enterprises became the living embodiment of the AG Business Flow Framework™. The transformation was not only visible in metrics but also felt in mindset.

Precision replaced panic.

Performance became predictable.

Discipline evolved into culture.

Final Quote: "Precision is not perfection. It is alignment with purpose."

Chapter 12: Building a Self-Sustaining Organization: The Roadmap to Maturity

AG Business Flow Framework™

"When systems think, leaders can lead."

1. From Management to Maturity

Every organization begins as a spark, an idea powered by people, purpose, and passion. As it grows, complexity multiplies. Decisions increase, systems stretch, and performance starts to depend more on individuals than on processes.

The real shift from management to maturity happens when clarity replaces urgency, when workflows are built not only to execute but also to anticipate, correct, and improve on their own.

A self-sustaining organization does not need constant supervision to succeed. It moves forward through alignment, intelligence, and accountability, creating a steady rhythm of progress that continues beyond any single leader or department.

This chapter represents the final stage of the AG Business Flow Framework™ where operations evolve into foresight and leadership rises from control to capability.

2. The Organization Maturity Ladder

Every organization's journey follows a predictable evolution, moving from reaction to prediction. Understanding this ladder of maturity helps leaders recognize not only where they stand, but what they must become.

Stage	Name	Core Behaviour	Leadership Style	Digital Capability
Stage 1	Reactive	Firefighting mode, progress depends on individuals	Directive and top-down	Manual reporting and scattered data
Stage 2	Controlled	Procedures exist but are centralized, with stability valued over speed	Managerial control	Departmental systems with limited automation
Stage 3	Integrated	Functions align and data begins to flow across departments	Collaborative leadership	ERP or CRM connection with shared dashboards
Stage 4	Adaptive	Teams learn and improve dynamically through data feedback	Coaching and enabling	Automation, analytics, and continuous feedback loops
Stage 5	Predictive	The organization anticipates challenges before they occur	Visionary and empowering	AI-driven insights and self-learning systems

At **Stage 5**, the organization becomes intelligent by design. Systems provide foresight, teams act with confidence, and leaders shift their energy from correction to creation, from solving problems to shaping the future.

When systems think, leaders can truly lead.

Mini-Case Example: From Control to Foresight

A regional engineering contractor moved from Stage 2 (Controlled) to Stage 4 (Adaptive) by integrating its estimation, job tracking, and billing systems into a single ERP dashboard. Within twelve months:

- Project turnaround time improved by 22%
- Rework reduced by 18%
- Invoice delay dropped by 50%

The outcome proved a universal truth: Process maturity is not automation. It is anticipation.

3. Leadership Commentary: The Digital Mindset and Culture of the Future

To achieve predictive maturity, leaders must evolve faster than their tools. Technology can enable efficiency, but only mindset and culture can sustain excellence.

> *"Digital transformation is not technology adoption, it is the leadership of anticipation."*

The digital-era leader embodies five key shifts, not in systems but in self:

- **From Ownership to Stewardship:** Lead purposefully, not possessively. Great leaders do not control systems, they nurture ecosystems.
- **From Data Access to Data Intelligence:** Value insight over volume. Information means little until it changes a decision.
- **From Supervision to Enablement:** Replace control with clarity and trust. Empowered teams outperform managed teams every time.
- **From Stability to Agility:** Treat change as rhythm, not risk. Adaptation becomes the organization's heartbeat.

- **From Compliance to Curiosity:** Create safety for experimentation and learning. Curiosity keeps innovation alive long after transformation is complete.

When these behaviours become cultural norms, digital transformation transcends software and becomes an organizational state of mind. Leaders no longer manage information, they amplify intelligence. The result is a culture where progress is not enforced, it is inspired.

4. The DNA of a Self-Sustaining Organization

Sustainability thrives at the intersection of clarity and capability. A truly mature organization functions like a living system, resilient, adaptive, and continuously learning. Its strength rests on five enduring foundations:

- **Purpose-Driven Strategy:** Vision defines every metric, every decision, and every direction. Purpose becomes the anchor that holds progress steady amid change.

- **Process Integration:** Sales, estimation, execution, and finance flow as one continuous value chain. No silos. No handover friction. Only seamless movement from opportunity to outcome.

- **Empowered People:** Decisions are made where information resides. Ownership replaces oversight, and empowerment replaces escalation.

- **Data Intelligence:** Information transforms into anticipation. The organization no longer asks "What happened?" but already knows "What happens next."

- **Cultural Resilience:** Values evolve without losing integrity. Adaptation becomes natural, and transformation becomes routine.

When these five foundations operate in harmony, maturity ceases to be a project and becomes a habit. That is the moment when organizations stop sustaining processes and start sustaining themselves.

5. The Five-Point Strategic Roadmap (2026 - 2030)

A roadmap for continuous maturity under the AG Business Flow Framework™.

2026 - Digitize and Integrate

Connect all operational systems such as CRM, ERP, finance, and project controls into a unified digital ecosystem. Enable real-time visibility and remove manual reporting delays.

> *Principle: If you cannot see it, you cannot improve it. Integration creates the foundation for predictability and ensures one version of truth across all departments.*

2027 - Empower and Educate

Train teams to think in systems instead of silos. Develop internal Process Champions who sustain digital tools and reinforce process discipline. Encourage decision-making autonomy within defined governance boundaries.

> *Outcome: Confidence grows when people understand the reason behind every workflow.*

2028 - Predict and Improve

Adopt AI-assisted forecasting, resource prediction, and risk analytics. Establish a Digital Improvement Office (DIO) to ensure continuous progress and structured review cycles.

> *Insight: Prediction replaces reaction only when learning becomes continuous. This is the year when intelligence*

becomes proactive and the organization starts to anticipate rather than adjust.

2029 - Institutionalize and Lead

Embed maturity into governance, strategy, and leadership development. Integrate the AG Business Flow Framework™ into annual planning and audit cycles. Ensure knowledge transfer through structured mentorship and innovation labs.

Outcome: Transformation stops being a project and becomes policy.

2030 - Legacy Through Learning

Build an organization that improves faster than its environment changes. At this stage, the company becomes self-correcting, where systems, people, and purpose operate in harmony.

Legacy Statement: Maturity is not an achievement, it is a rhythm, a continuous alignment between vision and velocity.

6. Process Integration: The Pulse of Predictive Maturity

A truly mature organization does not operate in silos, it moves as a single, synchronized organism. Each process amplifies the next, creating a continuous feedback loop of clarity, action, and foresight.

Function	Integration Focus	Outcome
Sales & Estimation	Unified opportunity and cost intelligence	Faster, data-backed bids
Planning & Execution	Linked schedules and dynamic Gantt dashboards	Real-time coordination and accountability

Function	Integration Focus	Outcome
Completion & Invoicing	Auto-synced billing triggers	Zero leakage and accelerated cash flow
Finance & Reporting	Predictive analytics and KPI dashboards	Early risk detection and proactive correction
Leadership & Review	Digital performance cockpit	Foresight-led decision-making

Integration transforms control into confidence and data into direction. When every process speaks the same digital language, the organization begins to think and act as one.

7. Checklist for Continuous Maturity

A maturity journey never truly ends, it evolves through reflection, review, and renewal. Use this checklist as a quarterly discipline to sustain foresight, alignment, and accountability across every function.

Focus Area	Key Question	Status (✓ / ✗)
Purpose Alignment	Is our vision translated into measurable outcomes?	
System Integration	Are sales, estimation, execution, and finance connected digitally?	
Digital Visibility	Can leadership access real-time insights without waiting for reports?	
Empowerment	Do teams make informed decisions independently and confidently?	
Knowledge Retention	Is expertise captured, documented, and easily retrievable?	
Learning Culture	Are failures consistently converted into learning cycles?	

Focus Area	Key Question	Status (✓ / ✗)
Predictive Readiness	Are analytics used to anticipate and prevent future risks?	
Leadership Continuity	Are we developing successors who will sustain the culture of discipline?	

Organizations that treat this checklist as a routine create a culture where progress becomes perpetual, not periodic. It is not a report, it reflects readiness.

> *Leadership Reflection: A mature organization does not chase growth, it cultivates it. Each review is not about correction but about continuous calibration toward excellence.*

8. The Future-Ready Organization

Tomorrow's leaders will not manage, they will orchestrate. They will blend digital precision with human depth, ensuring that technology serves people rather than replaces them.

A future-ready organization is defined by four enduring behaviours:

- **Thinks Systemically** - sees connections, not compartments.
- **Acts Adaptively** - adjusts course without losing direction.
- **Learns Continuously** - turns feedback into foresight.
- **Leads Collectively** - replaces hierarchy with harmony.

Technology provides data, but wisdom converts it into direction. That is the defining difference between digitalisation and maturity.

> *Final Reflection: The future belongs to organizations that align clarity with curiosity and technology with trust.*

Predictive maturity is not the end of transformation, it is the beginning of timeless relevance.

9. Conclusion: Process Maturity Is Not Automation, It's Anticipation

The journey to a self-sustaining organization is not about perfecting control, it is about designing foresight. Automation may increase speed, but maturity multiplies understanding.

A predictive organization senses risks before they surface, learns from every outcome, and aligns every action with purpose. Its systems think, its people lead, and its culture evolves.

Process maturity is not automation, it is anticipation. It is the ability to act before the problem arrives, to improve before the failure occurs, and to sustain excellence before urgency demands it.

When foresight becomes culture and discipline becomes instinct, the organization transcends survival and achieves perpetual relevance.

Final Closing Paragraph

The AG Business Flow Framework concludes here not as a system but as a state of mind. Its purpose was never just to document processes, but to awaken discipline, clarity, and foresight across every layer of the organization.

Maturity is not a milestone, it is a motion. Every project, every meeting, and every decision becomes a small rehearsal for greatness when **purpose, people, and process move in perfect rhythm**.

ATTRIBUTION & REFERENCE NOTES

This book references several globally recognised professional standards and practices to illustrate industry concepts. All intellectual property rights remain with their respective organisations.

AACE International. Concepts in estimation classification are adapted from AACE International Recommended Practice No. 18R-97: "Cost Estimate Classification System – As Applied in Engineering, Procurement, and Construction for the Process Industries." Used here for educational and illustrative purposes only.

PMI® / PMBOK® Guide. Project management process groups and estimation methods are discussed with reference to the Project Management Institute's A Guide to the Project Management Body of Knowledge (PMBOK® Guide). Used under fair use for commentary and academic reference. PMBOK® and PMI® are registered trademarks of the Project Management Institute, Inc.

ISO 9001:2015. Mentions of document control and quality management practices are based on publicly available principles from ISO 9001:2015 – Quality Management Systems – Requirements, used for educational explanation.

Lean Six Sigma. Concepts of process improvement and variation control are referenced from Lean and Six Sigma methodologies as open professional frameworks.

Disclaimer: The interpretations, explanations, and applications presented in this book are original to the author and do not represent official publications, endorsements, or guidance from AACE International, PMI, ISO, or any related body.

ABOUT THE AUTHOR

Arun Govindaraj is an Estimation and Commercial Operations Leader with nearly two decades of experience across Oil & Gas, Petrochemical, and Power sectors.

He has led estimation, project control, and commercial teams for structural, piping, and skid fabrication, as well as for maintenance, rotating equipment services, thermal coating, and field operations. His professional experience includes delivering complex engineering projects, integrating cost systems, and improving organisational reliability through process discipline.

Arun developed the AG Business Flow Framework[TM], a practical leadership model that helps organisations build reliability through structured process and foresight. His philosophy "Precision in Vision, Power in Execution" reflects his belief that process discipline is not control but clarity in motion.

A certified PMP and ISO internal auditor, Arun has engineered automation that connects Outlook and Excel through VBA, enabling data transfer and calculation without manual effort. He also developed a complete estimation system within ERP that unifies all service categories, ensuring consistency and transparency across every project.

When not writing or developing framework, he focuses on mentoring teams, advancing process maturity, and exploring AI-driven solutions for project and estimation management.

A NOTE TO THE READER

Thank you for reading Precision in Vision: Building a Process-Driven Organization.

Every Framework and reflection in this book come real projects, people, and lessons learned through years of in the field.

If these ideas help you lead with more clarity, reliability, and foresight, then the purpose of this book is fulfilled.

Reliability is not in one decision. It is built when process becomes culture and leadership becomes habit.

Wit discipline and clarity, every organisation can build own rhythm of precision.

Arun Govindaraj

LinkedIn: https://www.linkedin.com/in/arungovindarajtrichy

Made in the USA
Middletown, DE
07 December 2025

24186199R00106